Mandalas for Beginners

Examples, Structures, Meditations and Rituals

Contact: www.HarryEilenstein.de
            Harry.Eilenstein@web.de
            Harry Eilenstein at youtube

Production and publishing house: BoD – Books on Demand, Norderstedt

ISBN: 9783753498997

Table of Contents

I   What is a Mandala?

From a purely geometric point of view, a mandala is a concentric pattern. In most cases, it consists of several concentric rings that have been divided into four quarters by a cross. However, there are also mandalas that consist of concentric squares, that is, squares that have been drawn inside each other and have the same center. The same thing exists with triangles, hexagons, etc., but the division into four is the most common.

From its content and from its use, a mandala is a symbolic map, a representation of the world. In it, the elements that make up the world appear in an arrangement that corresponds to the relationships among these elements.

Such mandalas can be very simple and may consist of only two elements, such as a circle symbolizing the soul and a ring around this circle representing the body. Another very simple mandala is the sun symbol, which consists of a circle (horizon) and a cross (the four cardinal points) in it.

However, a mandala can also be very complex and contain many dozens of elements systematically arranged in it.

The best known are probably the mandalas of Tibetan Buddhists, which are often made of colored sand scattered on a smooth surface and are usually about 3m·3m in size. Very similar mandalas are also painted by the Navaho Indians – also from colored sand. Further mandalas are found with the Indians, rudimentarily also in the Mesopotamian cultures in the middle Neolithic period and with some other peoples.

Often one finds Mandalas in the myths of the most different peoples, which are described in the myths, but nowhere as mandalas, i.e. pictorially represented or explicitly as such designated.

These mandalas form the basis for meditations, for rituals and sometimes also for oracles. These mandalas are usually also an important part of the cult.

II The Structure of Mandalas

Mandalas have a very systematic and also symmetrical structure. The elements contained in such a mandala are usually also found in the myths andin the cult of the tradition in question.

II 1. The Center

Just about every mandala has a center. This center is the essence of being, the source of the world, the root of life, the origin of souls, the quintessence of the alchemists, the Tao of the Chinese, the beginning and the end, the Alpha and the Omega, the "Great Mystery" of the Dakota, a deity, the sun, the soul …

Since the mandalas commonly used in cult almost always represent the world as a whole, the essence of these mandalas, that is, their center, is the Kether (Unity) of the Kabbalists, the Nirvana (emptiness) of the Buddhists, the Satori (enlightenment) in Zen, the One God in Judaism, Christianity and Islam, etc.

Of course, one can also make mandalas on a certain, limited theme – their center then is the essence of this theme. Such subordinated mandalas can be found especially in the sand paintings of the Navaho Indians and in the Tibetan Buddhist mandalas.

This center is in each mandala the goal of the meditations, dream journeys and rituals connected with it.

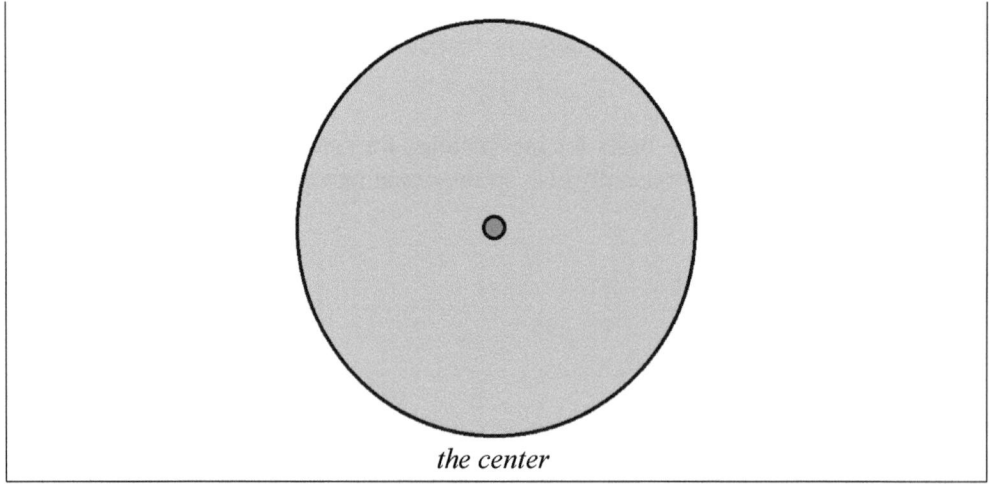

the center

II 2. The Concentric Rings

The rings are concentric around the "source-circle" in the center. In place of the rings sometimes squares, hexagons or other regular shapes are used – sometimes also e.g. combinations of circles and squares.

- Seen from the inside out, these circular rings represent the steps of development, the stages of creation, the unfolding of the world, the incarnation of the soul, etc.
In Kabbalah, this direction is called the "Lightning Ray of Creation."

- Looking from the outside inward, these circular rings represent the steps of knowledge, the sections of enlightenment, the dissolution of the world, the excarnation of the soul, etc.
In Kabbalah, this direction is called the "Serpent of Wisdom".

Thus, the rings symbolize the path between inside and outside, between God and the world, soul and body, consciousness and matter, etc.

The circular rings are, so to speak, the consequences of the first cause: the circles that form in water when you throw a stone into it …

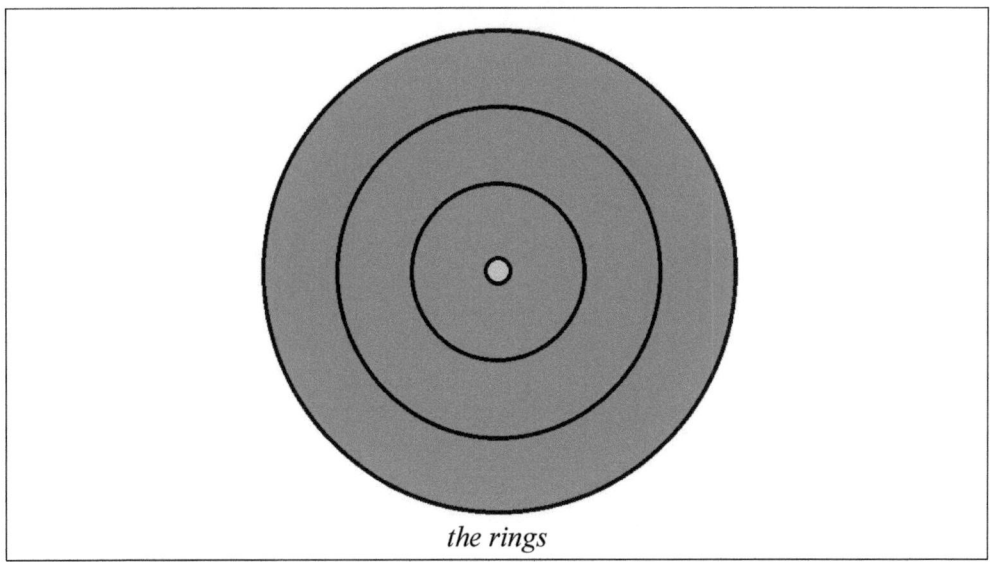

the rings

II 3. The Subdivision of the Rings

In some mandalas, the individual rings are once again subdivided into further areas, which all belong to the ring in question, but whose qualities show clear differences.

These subdivisions usually have the same number in each circular ring – in the example below there are three rings with three subareas each.

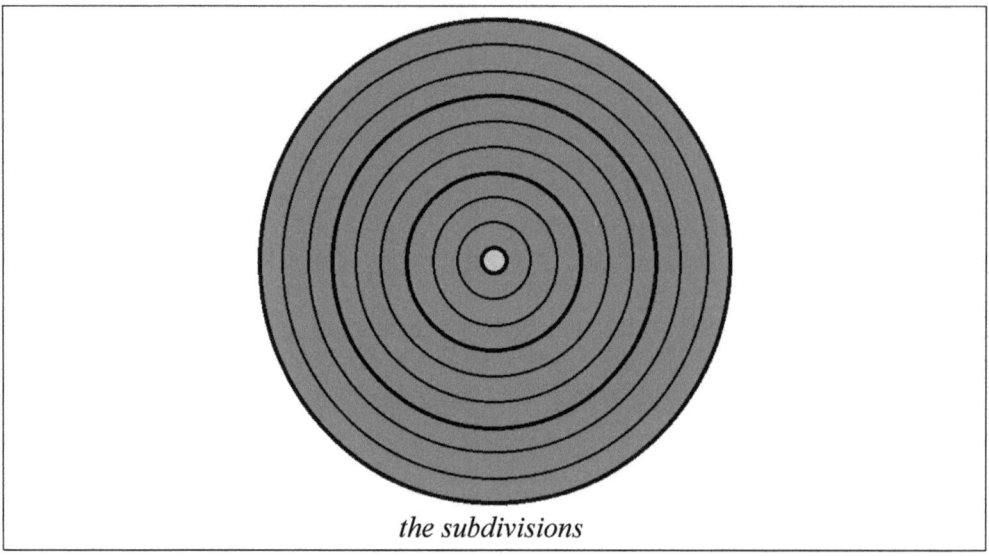

the subdivisions

II 4. The Outer Ring

The outer ring is the antithesis of the center: it is the being that has become concrete, unity that has become multiplicity, the will of the Creator that has become form, the form of life, the body of men, the raw and unpurified prima materia of the alchemists, the completed work, the outer form …

It is the Malkuth of the Kabbalists, the Samsara (form) of the Buddhists, the creation …

The outer ring is the place where every meditation, every dream journey and every ritual related to the mandala begins.

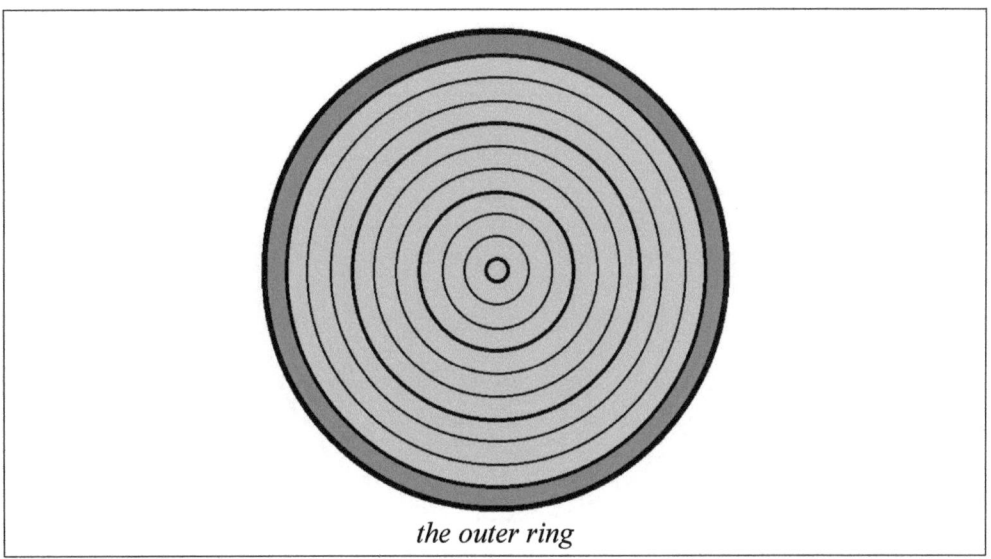

the outer ring

II 5. The Surrounding Space

In some mandalas there is still a surrounding space around the actual mandala. In it sometimes the forces of transformation are represented, sometimes also the causes for the occupation with such a mandala and the like.

These scenes are quite important, but they do not belong to the mandala proper – they are the outer space, the environment, the influences, the effects and the like. However, in some rituals this surrounding space plays an essential role.

Usually this surrounding space is not represente by a ring, but by other geometrical forms or even just by pictures.

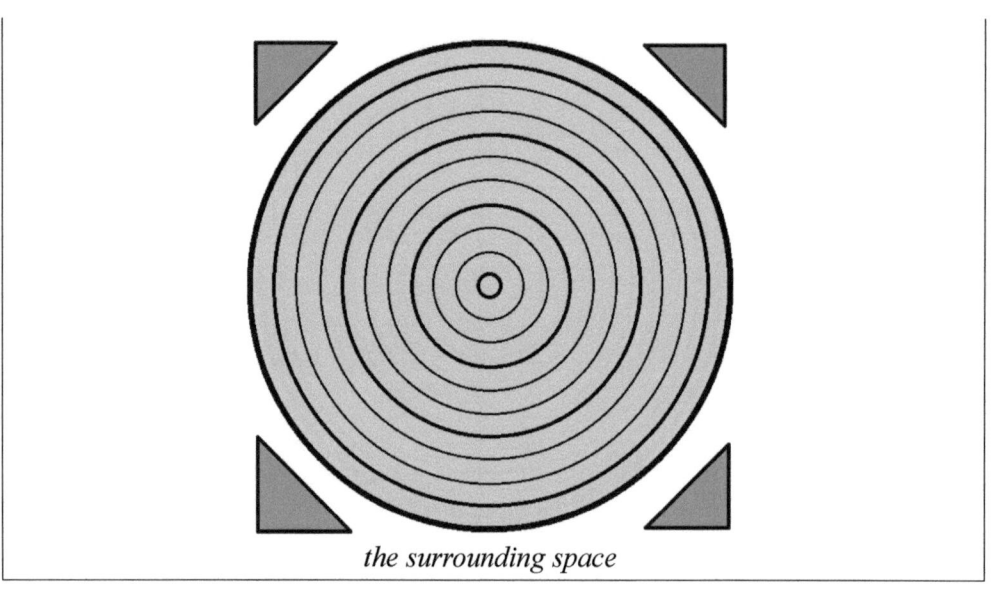

the surrounding space

II 6. The Directions

As a rule, a mandala has four directions. In this case the mandala consists either of concentric circular rings or of concentric squares.

However, three, five, six or other "exotic" numbers of directions are also possible. The number of directions depends on how many basic elements the world consists of in the mythology used:

the directions in the mandala		
Number	*Culture*	*Elements*
1	general	man
2	general	man and woman
3	colors	red, blue, yellow
4	western culture	fire, water, air, earth
5	China	fire, water, air, wood, metal
6	planets	Moon, Mercury, Venus, Mars, Jupiter, Saturn (Sun = center)
7	planets	Moon, Mercury, Venus, Sun, Mars, Jupiter, Saturn
8	I Ching trigrams	sky, earth, mountain, lake, fire, water, wind, thunder
etc.		

By the directions, the mandala is divided into different qualities that represent the possible states of beings and things in the world. This means that one can take different paths to the center of the mandala.

One starts with the path whose quality is easiest for oneself, but in order to be able to enter the next inner circular ring, it is necessary to be able to walk the other paths in this ring also – at least to some extent.

An example of a mandala without directional divisions (i.e. with number of direction "1") is a city in which there is a sun temple in the center, which one strives to reach.

11

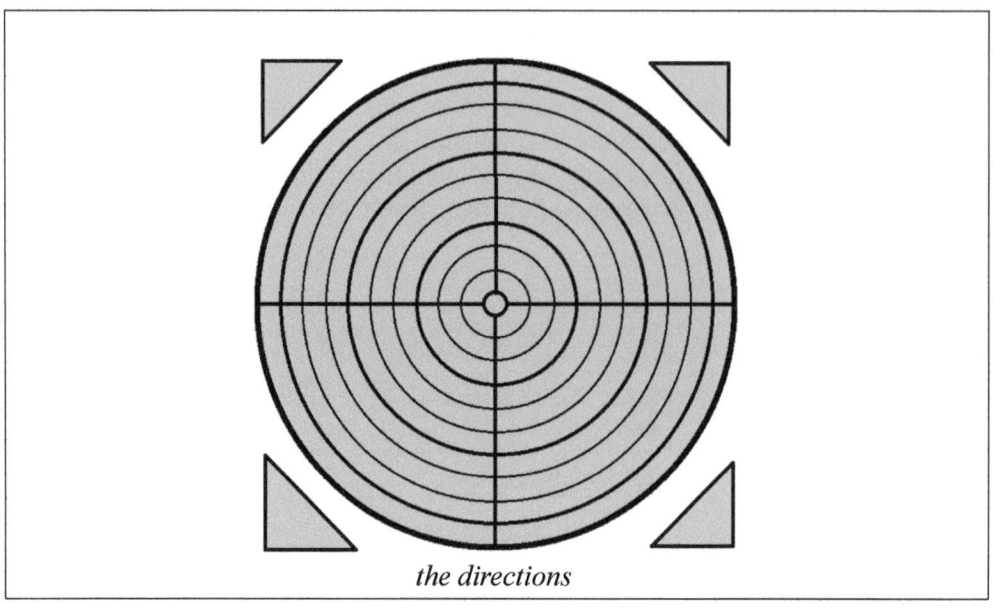

the directions

The mandala shown here consists of the following elements:

- the center (circle)
- three rings
- three subordinate rings in each main ring
- the outer ring
- the division into four directions
- the surrounding space (four triangles)

II 7.   The City on the Hill

A mandala is sometimes regarded as a city:

> - On the outside area are the gardens, fields and pastures, and the cemeteries.

> - The city is surrounded by a wall on the outside.

> - In each of the four directions of the mandala there is a gate in this city wall.

> - From these gates an avenue leads to the gate in the inner city walls, which surround the rings.

> - Each ring is filled with buildings.

> - In the center is the temple of the deity or the palace of the king.

Sometimes each ring is also on a higher level than the ring that surrounds it – so you have to climb a staircase in front of each city gate.

Such "mandala hill cities" have also been architecturally realized as temples such as in Angkor Wat in Cambodia, in Wat Arun in Bangkok and in Borobudur on Java. There you can enter a mandala and sit down physically and meditate or perform a ritual in it at any place you could otherwise only see as a picture or in a dream journey.

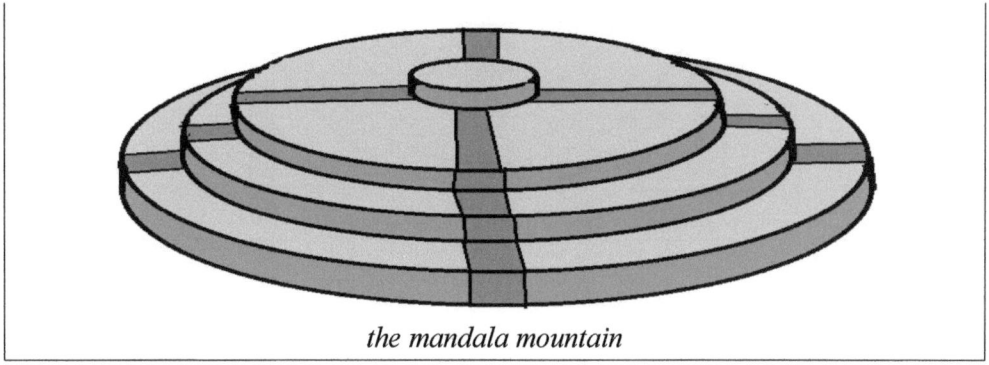

the mandala mountain

II 8.   Complementary additions

   In some mandalas there is also a complementary opposition in the center such as "man and woman", "god and goddess", "yin and yang", etc., which represent two aspects of the world. Usually these two poles are united – they are, for example, the inner man and the inner woman in one's psyche or the yin/yang symbol.
   In order to experience the center, the last step in these mandalas is to unite these two poles. In this case, the innermost ring is only two-divided and not four-divided. The two outer rings with their tree subdivisions each correspond for example to the four elements, the inner ring with its three subdivisions to Yin and Yang and the center to Tao.
   This kind of change of the number of directions does sometimes occur in mandalas, but it is rather rare.

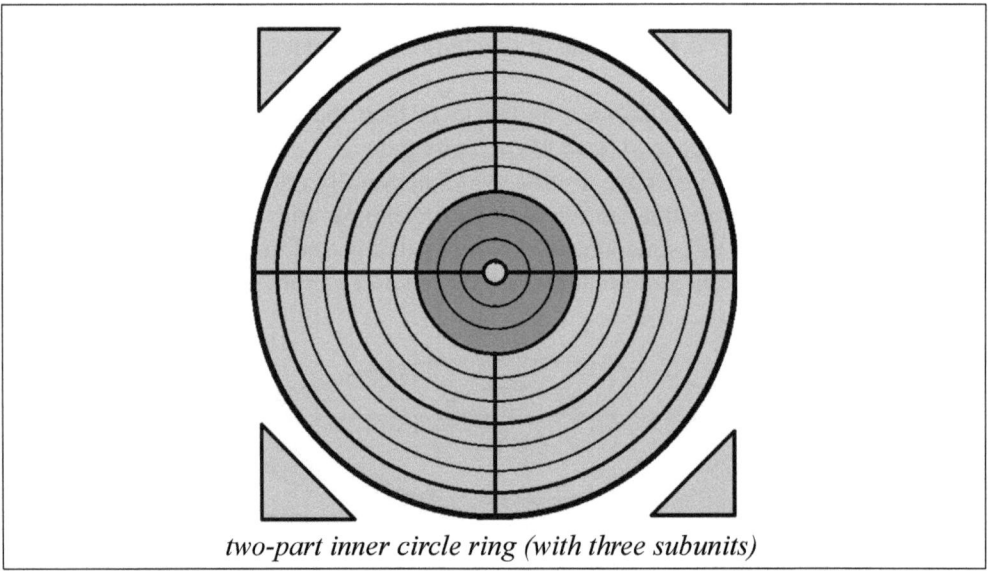

two-part inner circle ring (with three subunits)

III Mandala Examples

There are a large number of mandalas, some of which are very different in their structure, quality and use. In this chapter, only a small part of them will be listed, since the only purpose of this chapter is to illustrate the great variety of mandalas.

III 1. The Four Elements and the Quintessence

One of the simplest mandalas consists only of the center as the symbol of the origin (quintessence) and the four elements as the expression of the potential of this origin. This mandala is the basis of the "Lesser Pentagram Ritual" and the "Greater Pentagram Ritual", among others.

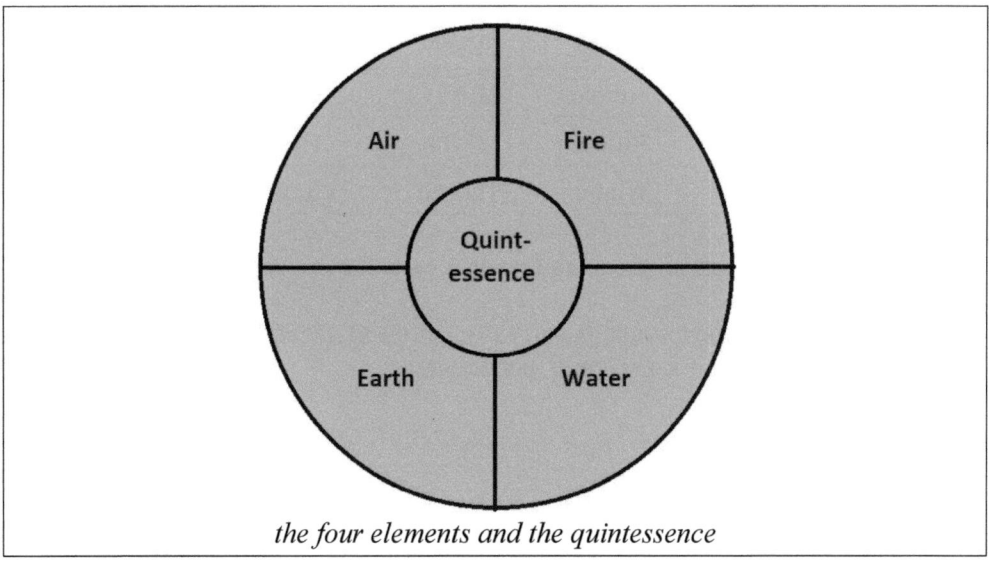

the four elements and the quintessence

III 2. The Four Cardinal Points and the Sun

This mandala looks very similar to the previous one, but it has a completely different inner dynamic. The Element Mandala is static, while the Sun Mandala is dynamic.

In the center of the sun mandala is the sun, by its position in the sky one can recognize the cardinal points, the times of day and the seasons. The four cardinal directions also correspond to the four elements and their arrangement in the pentagram ritual. The dynamic aspect of this mandala is the solar cycle, the wheel of the year, the sequence of the seasons. This sequence runs clockwise in this mandala. This sequence is, among other things, also a correspondence to the life of a human being and to the grain cycle.

The analogies of the circle of the year					
Direction	*Day*	*Year*	*Life*	*Grain*	*Element*
East	Morning	Spring	Birth	Sowing	Air
South	Noon	Summer	Life	Growth	Fire
West	Evening	Autumn	Dying	Harvest	Water
North	Night	Winter	Death	Storage	Earth

These are by no means all the analogies that exist for this mandala of the wheel of the year.

The variety of analogies, symbols and associations to a mandala shows how important it is and how firmly it is anchored in a culture.

16

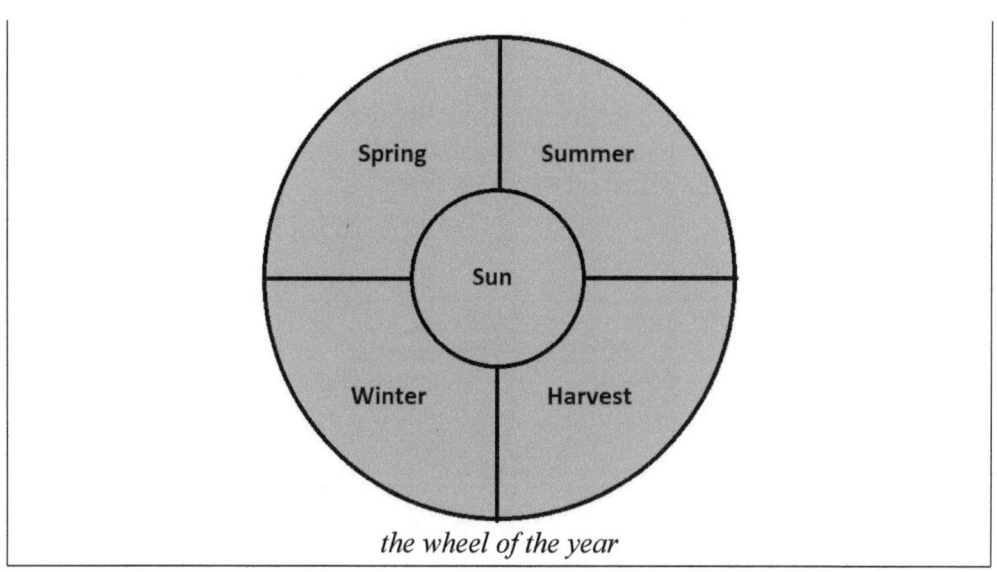

the wheel of the year

III 3.   The Zodiac

The zodiac is also a dynamic mandala, i.e. the outer areas represent a circular movement, which is divided into twelve "phases" in the zodiac. "Earth" here does not signify the element, but the planet on which we live.

The movement of the sun through the zodiac here runs counterclockwise: Aries – Taurus – Gemini, etc.

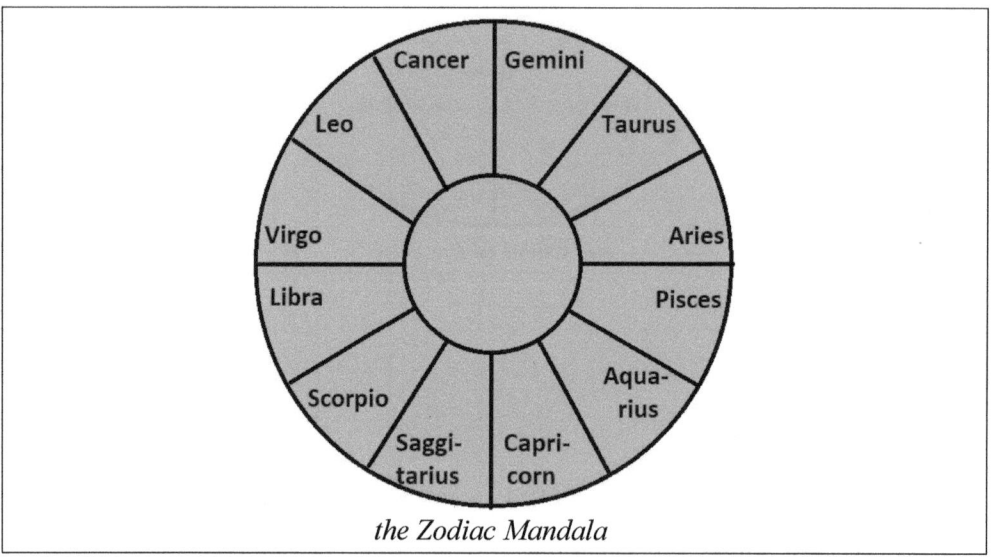

the Zodiac Mandala

It is possible to combine this mandala with the mandala of the four seasons, since both show the phases of the wheel of the year.

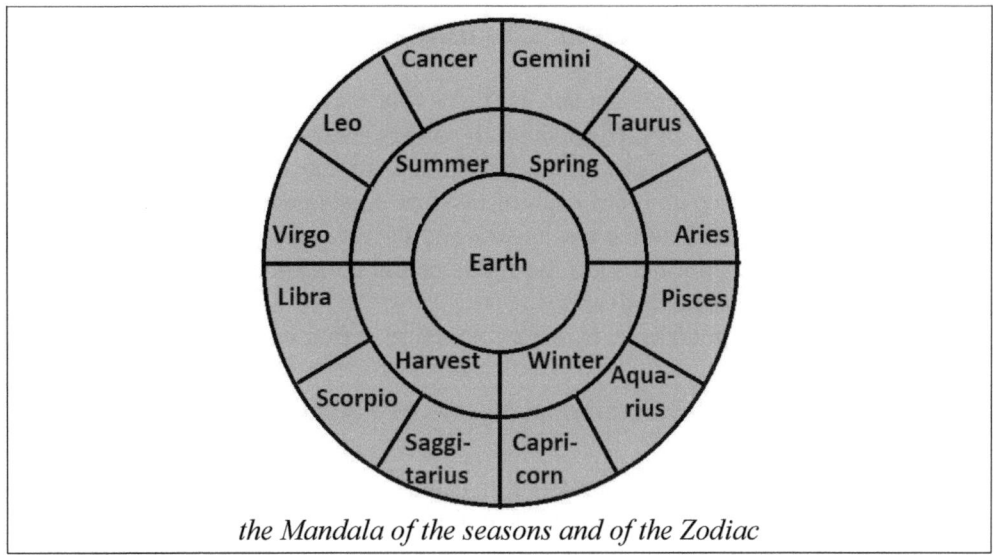

the Mandala of the seasons and of the Zodiac

The two rings of this mandala are no proper mandala-division, i.e. the two rings are not two steps.

The four seasons consist of three signs of the zodiac each – or, to put it more correctly, the four seasons are poolings of three signs of the zodiac each. The zodiac is a natural division – the four seasons are a man-made division.

III 4.   The elementary particles

There are exactly twelve elementary particles that make up our world. Just as the signs of the zodiac are composed of three dynamics ("cardinal", "fixed", "mutable") each of the four elements (fire, water, air, earth), so the elementary particles are composed of the three magnitudes each of the four fundamental particles. The exact assignment of the elements to the two quarks and the electron and the neutrino is still unclear – but this does not question the fundamental correspondence of the elementary particle system with the zodiac.

The following corresponddence is just a conjecture, a first working hypothesis.

Elementary particles and Zodiac			
elementary particles *Zodiac*	heavy elementary particles *heavy elements*	up-quark group *water*	up-quark *Cancer*
			charm-quark *Scorpio*
			top-quark *Pisces*
		down-quark group *earth*	down-quark *Capricorn*
			strange-quark *Taurus*
			bottom-Quark *Virgo*
	light elementary particles *light elements*	electron group *Air*	electron *Libra*
			muon *Aquarius*
			tauon *Gemini*
		neutrino group *Fire*	electron neutrino *Aries*
			muon neutrino *Leo*
			tauon neutrino *Sagittarius*

Possibly the Higgs boson, which gives mass to the elementary particles, corresponds to the center of this mandala – but this is uncertain.

It is also uncertain how the correct assignment of the twelve elementary particles to the twelve outer compartments of this mandala would look like. If the correct asignment of the elementary particles to the Zodiak would be known, then one could fill in the names of the elementary particles in this rather empty mandala.

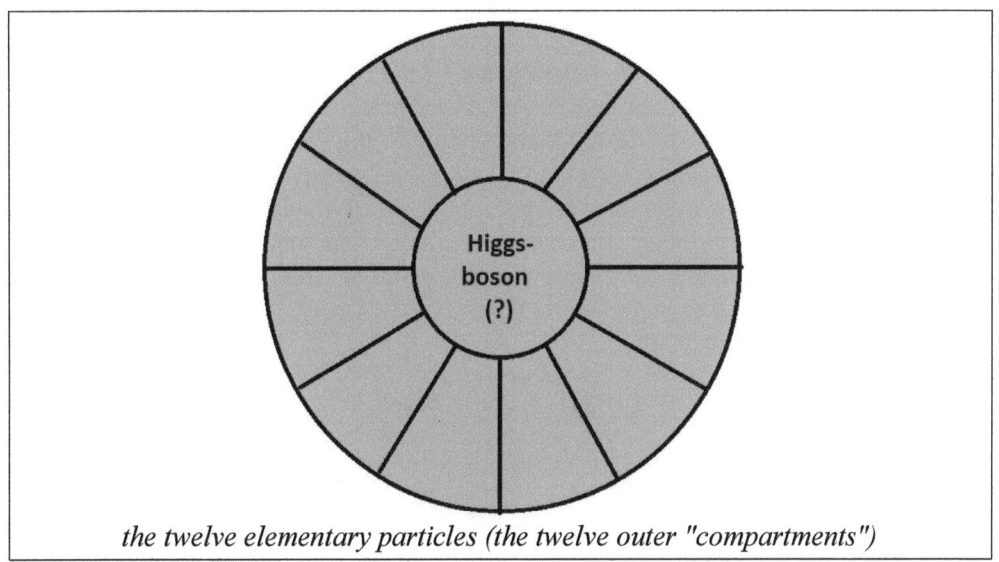

the twelve elementary particles (the twelve outer "compartments")

III 5.   The Superstring

The zodiac is such a fundamental part of our world that it is also found as the basic structure of all elementary particles. This basic structure is represented mathematically as a circularly vibrating "string", why this structure is called "string" or because of its great inner symmetry also "superstring". These strings are also known as "Heisenberg's spin chains". They are divided into twelve parts like the zodiac and are hollow inside, i.e. they are empty in their center, thus "only space".

They oscillate in such a way that always one of the twelve fields is "above" and the following field is "below". Each area vibrates alternately "up" and "down" – so there are always alternately the six fields corresponding to the elements water and earth in the zodiac or the six fields corresponding to the elements fire and air "up". This alternation is represented in the graphic by light and dark fields.

In the context of this book, the twelve-field division of the superstrings shows above all that mandalas are not only a concept of human thought, but that nature is constructed at its roots also in the form of mandalas.

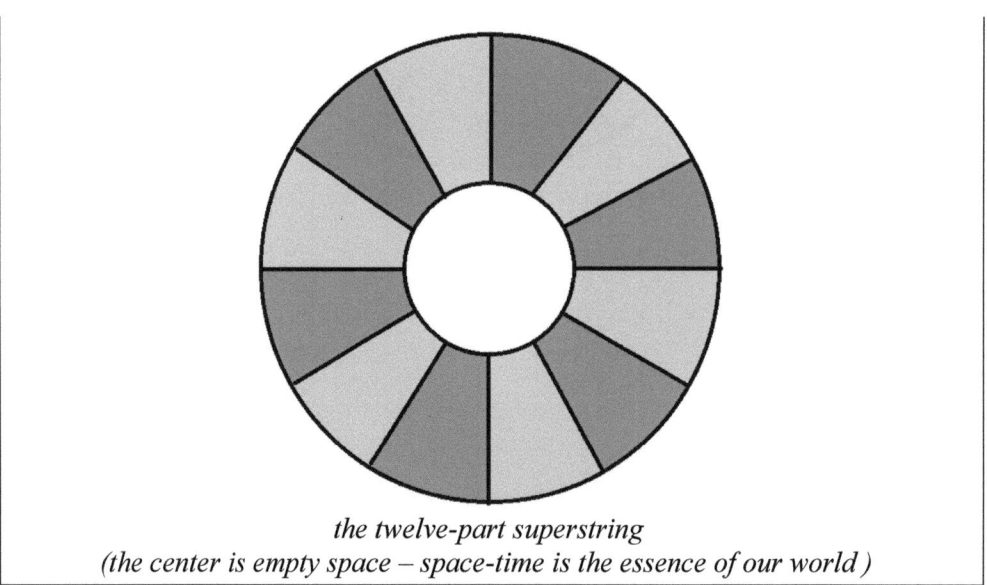

the twelve-part superstring
(the center is empty space – space-time is the essence of our world)

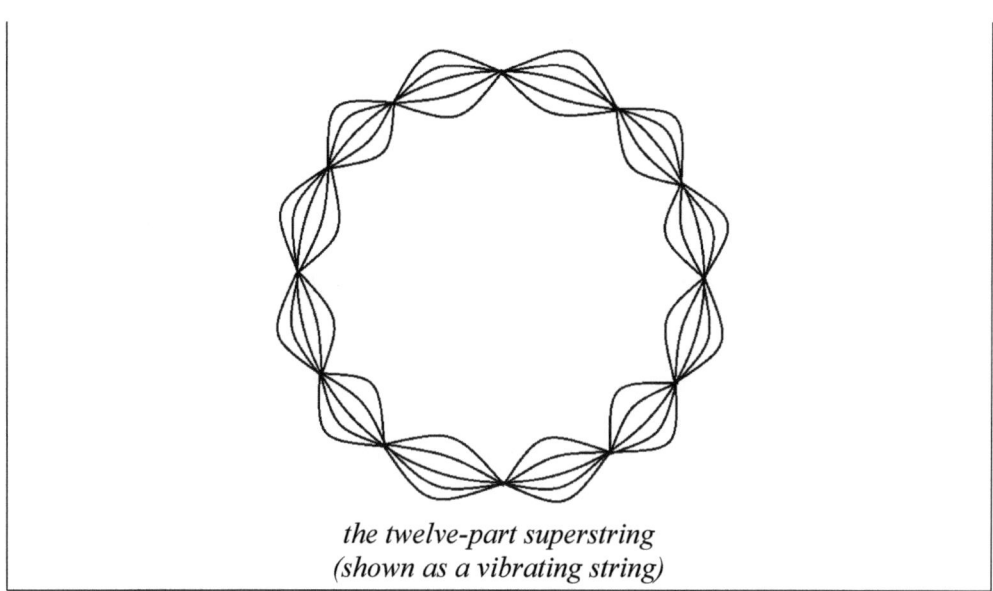

the twelve-part superstring
(shown as a vibrating string)

III 6. The Five Dhyani Buddhas

In Buddhism, there is a mandala consisting of five Buddhas that tell Buddha's life story:

- Buddha, as "Amithaba," contemplated the world in his meditation.

- Since he realized that the world is a unity at its core, he lost all fear and was therefore called "Amoghasiddhi".

- From the realization of the unity he decided to help all beings to this insight, because then he himself would also be the happiest - after all he himself is also a part of this unity of all beings. Thereupon he was called "Akshobhya".

- So he began to teach his realizations and the way to them as "Vairocana" - that is the center of the life of the Buddha and also of the Man-dala.

- In order to facilitate people's attainment of enlightenment, as "Ratnasambhava" he gave them himself as an example ("Buddha") and his teaching ("Dharma") and founded the monastic order ("Sangha").

Buddha's Biography Mandala			
Name	*Direction*	*Attitude*	*Meaning*
Amithaba	west	hands in lap	contemplation
Amoghasiddhi	north	left palm forward	fearlessness
Akshobhya	east	right hand tip on earth	determination
Vairocana	center	gesture: turning of the wheel	Teachings
Ratnasambhava	south	right hand in giving gesture	Initiations

This mandala is obviously a dynamic mandala, as it represents a development. A special feature of this mandala is that it is not concentric, but simply focuses on Buddha's teachings as the most important phase of life.

Strictly speaking, the representation of the five Dhyani Buddhas should therefore actually not be called "mandala", but "graphic", because there is no concentric-symmetrical structure.

24

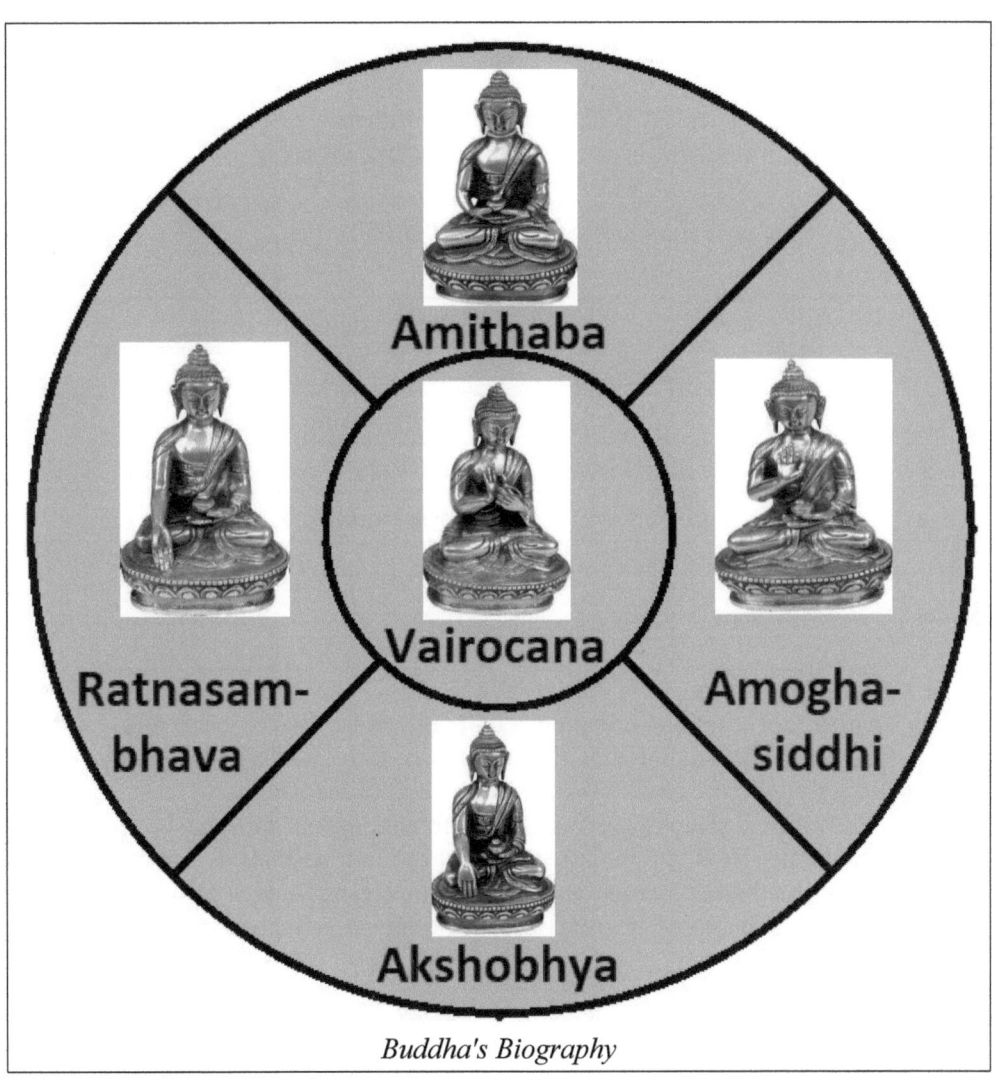

Amithaba

Ratnasam-
bhava

Vairocana

Amogha-
siddhi

Akshobhya

Buddha's Biography

III 7. The Sweat Lodge Mandala

The Sweat Lodge Mandala is actually a three-dimensional mandala consisting of the seven directions that have been common in ancient cultures:

The Seven Directions		
Direction	*Being*	*Quality*
west	Snake	power, seeing the small
north	Great Bear	independence, seeing oneself
east	Eagle	clarity, seeing the large
south	White Buffalo Woman	community, seeing the others
above	Grandfather Sky	responsibility, to bear others
unten	Grandmother Earth	trust, to be borne by others
center	Great Mystery	life

The four animals represent abilities, attitudes and ways of looking on the world and on life, which are contrast complements (eagle and snake; bear and buffalo). Grandfather Sky and Grandmother Earth are two more fundamental beings – they form the background. The Great Mystery is the heart of the whole.

Because these three groups have "roots of different depths," they can be represented as concentric circles. It is important to note that the four animals do not have a fixed assignment to grandfather heaven and grandmother earth – even though snake and buffalo have rather feminine qualities and eagle and bear embody rather masculine qualities.

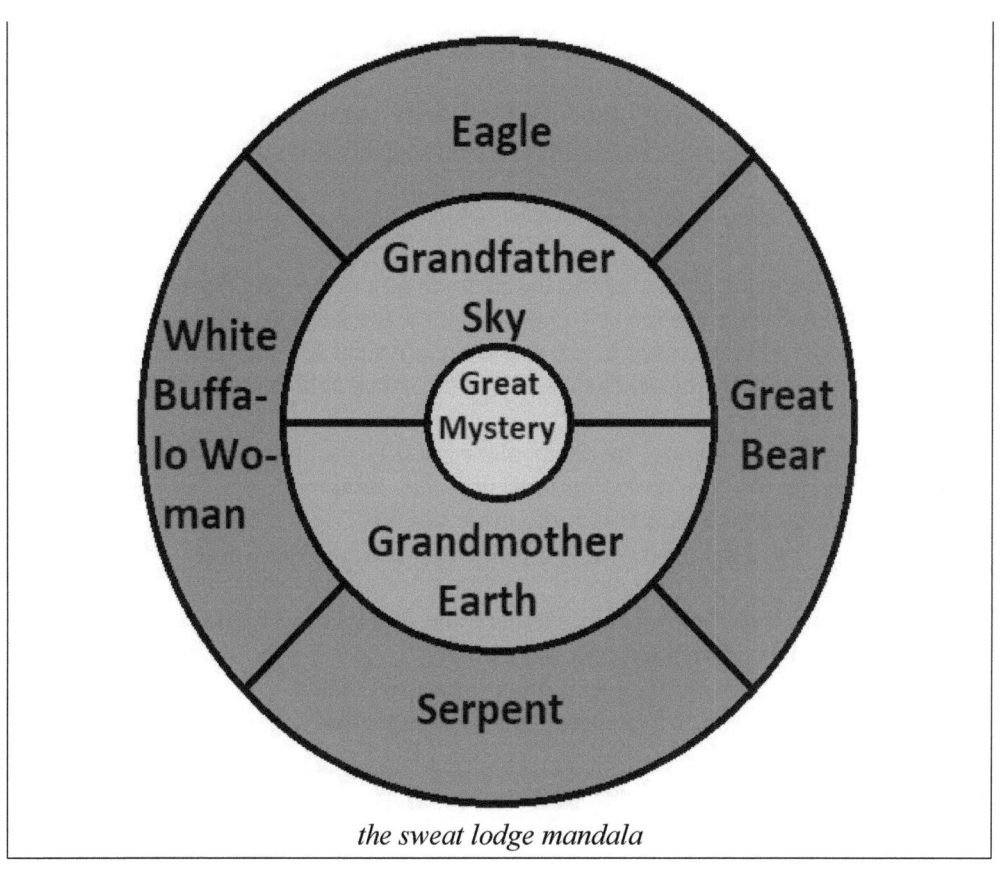

the sweat lodge mandala

III 8. The Chakra Mandala

The chakras are the "organs" of the life force body and the kundalini is the life force circuit in this life force body. The chakras are arranged in a symmetrical structure:

- In the center is the heart chakra, which contains a person's identity.

- In the solar plexus below the heart chakra and in the throat chakra above the heart chakra lies the self-expression, i.e. the feelings:
  - In the solar plexus, this is the physical self-expression.
  - In the throat chakra, this is the social self-expression.

- In the hara below the solar plexus and in the third eye above the throat chakra lies the concretization of desires, i.e., thinking:
  - In the hara, this is the inner stability.
  - In the third eye, this is the orientation in the world.

- In the root chakra below the hara and in the crown chakra above the third eye lies the experiencing, i.e. perception:
  - In the root chakra, this is physical contact.
  - In the crown chakra, this is the spiritual contact.

The Chakra Symmetry			Symmetry			
Chakra	*Function*	*Basic quality*				
crown chakra	spiritual contact	contact				
third eye	orientation	concretization				
throat chakra	social self-expression	impulse				
heart chakra	identity	identity				
solar plexus	physical self-expression	impulse				
hara	inner stablity	concretization				
root chakra	physical contact	contact				

The chakra mandala is one of the rare mandalas that consist of two halves instead of four quarters:

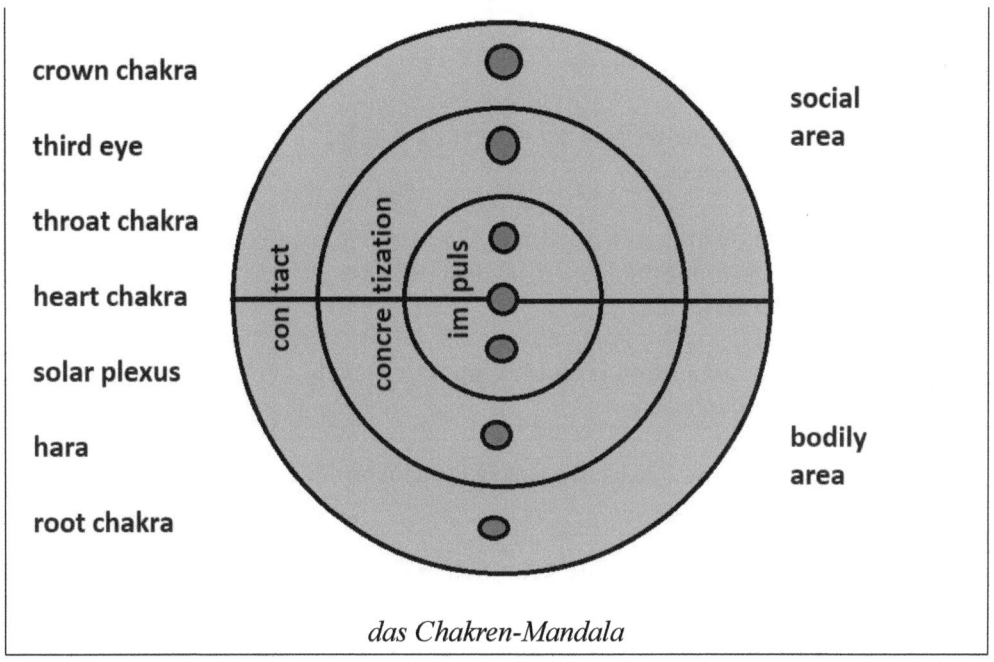

das Chakren-Mandala

The chakra mandala:

The center is the heart chakra.

The inner ring are the general desires: solar plexus and throat chakra.
The middle ring are the concrete desires: hara and third eye.
The outer ring are the contacts: root chakra and crown chakra.

The upper half is the social realm (outside)-
The lower half is the physical realm (inner).

III 9. The Tree of Life Mandala

The tree of life is a "3-step system":

    - In the beginning there is the world as a whole.
        => 1 element

    - Then this world is divided into God's unity, the diversity of the material world and the connection and dynamics between these two poles.
        => 3 elements

    - Next, this connection is divided into three levels.
        => 5 elements

    - Finally, each of these three stages is again divided into three "sub-stages".
        => 11 elements

This eleven-part structure is usually represented as a "tree" and named with Hebrew names. These eleven elements ("Sephiroth") correspond among other things to the eleven planets.

The Kabbalistic Tree of Life			
Tree of Life	*No.*	*Name*	*Planet*
	1	Kether	Pluto
	2	Chokmah	Neptune
	3	Binah	Uranus
	D	Da'ath	Saturn
	4	Chesed	Jupiter
	5	Geburah	Mars
	6	Tiphareth	Sun
	7	Netzach	Venus
	8	Hod	Mercury
	9	Yesod	Moon
	10	Malkuth	Earth

The Sephirah Da'ath is considered "invisible" or "hidden" in classical Kabbalah and therefore has not been given a number, which is why it is cited here with a "D" instead of a number.

This structure can be found in everything from a vacuum cleaner to the classical ballet to the German Constitution, which clearly shows that it is a universally valid structure.

You may see my books "Kursus der Praktischen Kabbalah" or "Blüten des Lebensbaumes I, II, III" for more details.

Since this graphic describes the unfolding of the multiplicity of the world from a unity, one can represent this "tree of life" also as Mandala.

The five main areas of this graphic (when applied to human beings) have the following correspondence, which is associated with certain experiences:

- A God:
      1. Kether: glistening white light.

- B Deities:
      2. Chokmah: storm of light
      3. Binah: community
      D. Da'ath: continuum

- C Souls:
      4. Chesed: incarnational memory
      5. Geburah: karma
      6. Tiphareth: soul

- D Psyche:
      7. Netzach: feelings
      8. Hod: thoughts
      9. Yesod: perception/memory

- E Body:
      10. Malkuth: body

The Tree of Life is first of all a mandala without divisions in the directions – it consists only of concentric circles.

The dark point in the centre of the graphic on the next page is the unity (God), then follow the three light circular rings of the deities, then the three dark circular rings of the soul, then the three light circular rings of the psyche and outside the dark circular ring of the body.

The different shades of gray ("light" and "dark") in this diagram have no meaning in terms of content, but shall only facilitate the comprehension of the mandala.

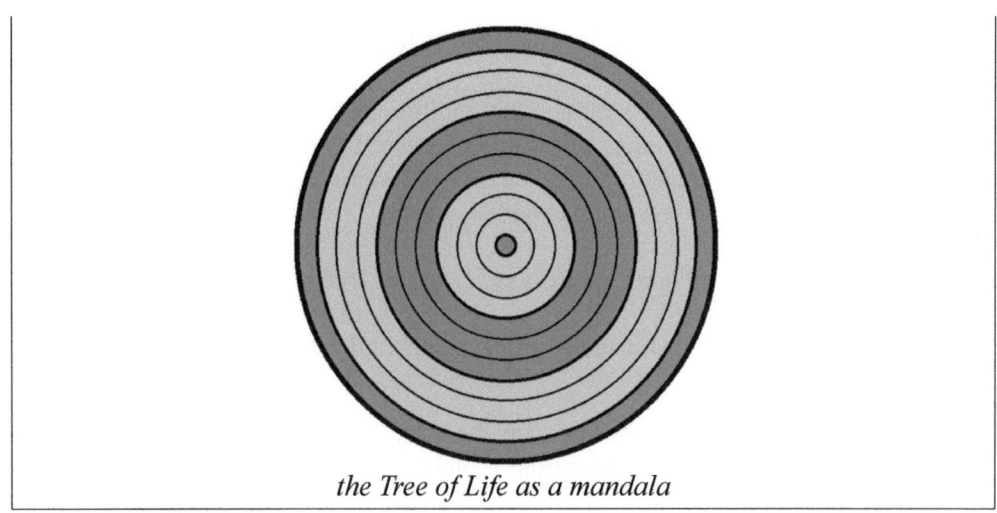

the Tree of Life as a mandala

The transitions between the main areas on the Tree of Life and so also in this mandala have traditonal names. These transitions are the broader black rings, i.e. the transitions between two different shades of gray.

These names are:

- The transition from the outer ring (body) to the three outer light rings (psyche): "threshold".

- The transition from the three light outer rings (psyche) to the three middle dark rings (soul): "trench".

- The transition from the three middle dark rings (soul) to the three inner light rings (deities): "abyss".

- The transition from the three light, inner rings (deities) to the dark circle in the center (God) has no traditional name, but could be called, for example, "last step".

These transitions, in a mandala ritual based on the Tree of Life, are where the greatest dynamism is found, as this is where a new realm is entered, new realizations emerge, and transformations are set in motion.

If this Tree of Life mandala is imagined as a city, the threshold, the trench, the abyss and the "last step" are the four gates through which one must pass within the city to reach the destination in the center. At these gates, "guards" are waiting, with whom one has to deal with – at the "trench", which leads from the psyche to the soul, this is e.g. one's own shadow, i.e. the repressed part of one's own psyche.

33

III 10. The Superstring Theory

The Tree of Life Mandala, which consists of a circle and ten circular rings, is also found in the most important place in physics: To describe a superstring, which is the basic structure of all elementary particles and all energy quanta in our world, one needs an eleven-dimensional mathematical model, which describes the eleven dimensions of our world.

This mathematical model corresponds exactly to the Tree of Life Mandala:

- The first and most original and fundamental dimension is time: the circle in the center (kether).

- The next three dimensions are the three "normal" space dimensions: the three inner light gray circular rings (Chokmah, Binah, Da'ath).

- The next three dimensions are not endlessly extended like the "normal" space dimensions, but tiny and therefore not perceptible in everyday life: the three middle dark gray circular rings (Chesed, Geburah, Tiphareth).

- The same applies also to the next three space dimensions which likewise appear only far below the size of an electron: the three outer light gray circular rings (Netzach, Hod, Yesod).

- Finally there is one last dimension which has the functionof summarizing the other ten dimensions: the outer circular ring (Malkuth).

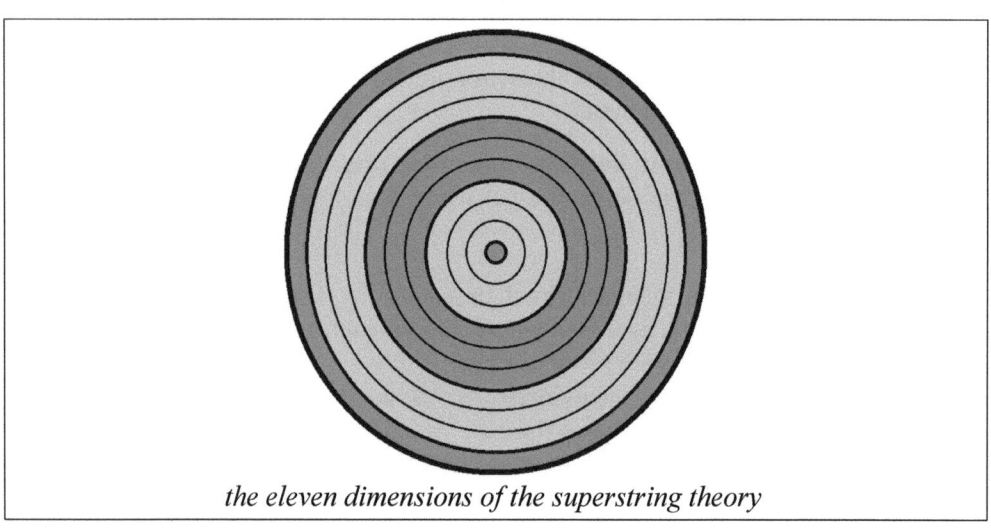

the eleven dimensions of the superstring theory

34

III 11. A Tarot Mandala

The Tarot cards have been derived from the Tree of Life. They are divided into three groups:

    - 1. group: 22 major arcana: They correspond to the paths on the Tree of Life, that is, the lines connecting the eleven "spheres".

    - 2. group: 56 minor arcana:

        - group 2. a)   The 16 court cards: They correspond to the four elements and appear in four forms each (king = fire aspect; queen = water aspect; knight = air aspect; knight = earth aspect).

        - group 2. b)   The 40 number cards: They correspond to the 10 Sephiroth (circles) on the Tree of Life (without Da'ath) and appear in four forms each, which correspond to the four elements.

Consequently, a four-part Tree of Life mandala can be made from the 40 number cards – but the Da'ath circular ring remains empty.

The practical use of this mandala is quite limited – it offers the possibility to combine one's knowledge of the Tarot and the Kabbalistic Tree of Life. If you want to perform a mandala ritual based on the Tree of Life, you can possibly use these 40 tarot cards to meditate on the path from the outside (multiplicity) to the inside (unity).

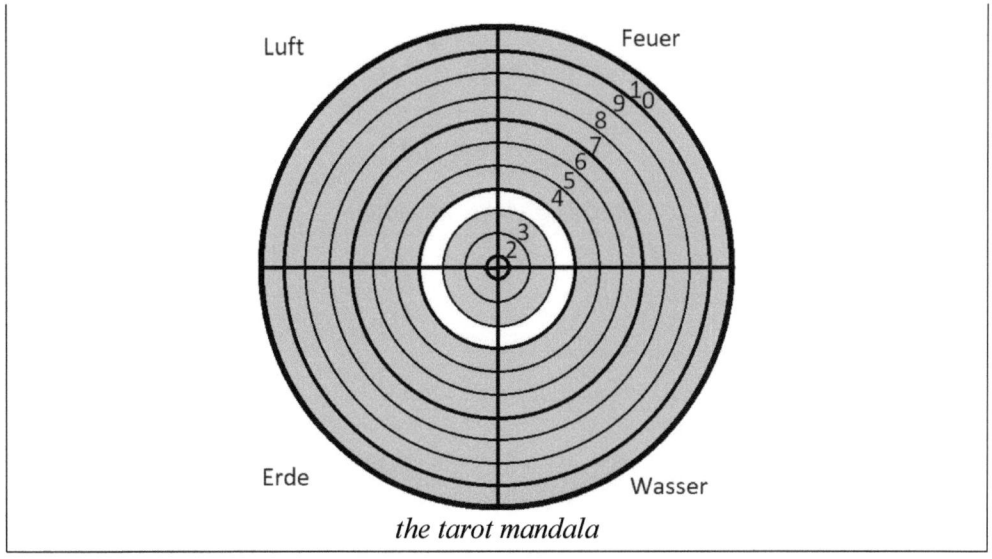

the tarot mandala

III 12. The Temple of the Sun

This is a meditation that originates from the Golden Dawn and is used to get in touch with one's own soul. This meditation consists of the following imagination:

- One walks through the desert towards a city => perimeter of the mandala.

- One enters the city through a gate => The city is the psyche.

- One goes through the city to the temple in its center. => The tempel is the heart chakra.

- There one invokes one's own soul and asks it to appear.

The mandala of this meditation is very simple:

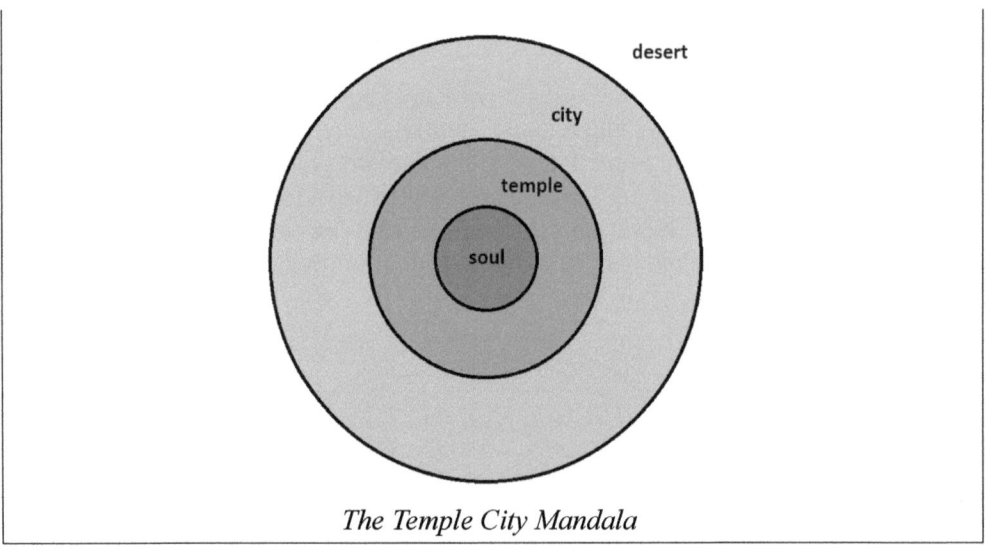

The Temple City Mandala

III 13. The Labyrinth

Another special form of the mandala is the path mandala, which consists of only one path like the labyrinth in the cathedral of Chartre. This labyrinth is also known in several simliar examples from the Neolithic Age.

Originally, these labyrinths were simply paths winding according to a certain pattern, representing the way from this world to the next.

The labyrinth consisting of a confusing variety of ways and sometimes even several obstacles has arisen only much later.

the otherworld path mandala (floor of the cathedral of Chatre)

III 14. The Relationship Mandala

The Relationship Mandala is a simple mandala that has resulted from my observations of my own psyche and from my consultations with other people. It contains a division of four and a division of two and a rather unusual inner structure.

This mandala consists of four areas:

1st area: The center is one's own soul with its decision to incarnate.

2nd area: The inner ring is divided in two and contains the image of the inner man and the image of the inner woman. These two images are the mirror images of one's own soul in the life force – since the life force is bipolar, two mirror images of the soul are created.

3rd area: When the psyche comes under great stress or when even a trauma arises, the two mirror images of the soul become polarized, giving rise to three kinds of polar extreme pairs: "addict and ascetic" or "perpetrator and victim" or "star and fan." This creates a total of four images: two polar distortions of the inner male image and two polar distortions of the inner female image. These four images are very formative for the structure and processes in the psyche.

4th area: A human one lives one of the four distorted images – e.g. the he-addict. However, the other three distorted images also want to be lived – which leads to projecting them onto other people and then performing a drama together with them. The theme of this drama is that which originally caused the polarization of the whole image of the inner women and the whole image of the inner men: lack, violence or disrespect.

In this drama, there are four clearly defined and fixed roles:

- The people with the same gender and the same polarization (in the example the he-addict) can become friends and "fellow sufferers".

- The people with the opposite sex and the same polarization (in the example the she-addict) can also become friends and "fellow sufferers".

- The people with the same sex and opposite polarization (in this example the he-ascetic) can become the enemy and competitor.

- The people of the opposite sex and polarization (in this example, the she-ascetic) are chosen to be relationship partners – and then form the core of the "life drama".

The she-addict, the he-ascetic and the she-ascetic play a role each in the drama of the he-addict – but he he-addict also plays a role in the dramas of the she-addict, the he-ascetic and the she-ascetic. Thus they perform together a complex social, common, and manyfold interwoven drama of "lack".

The healing of this mandala consists of three steps:

- First, one recognizes that the "actors in one's own drama" take on roles that one carries within oneself, and that one also takes on roles that the others carry within themselves. Then, with a symbolic gesture, one takes these roles, i.e. these projected inner images back into oneself – which is the greatest step of this healing.

- Secondly, one unites the two polarized pairs of distorted images with each other, whereby one finds again the two whole mirror images of one's own soul: the inner man and the inner woman.

- Thirdly, the two healed mirror images unite with each other, by which one's own soul becomes visible – this usually happens spontaneously and without one's own intervention.

A detailed description of this mandala may be found in my book "Das Beziehungs-Mandala".

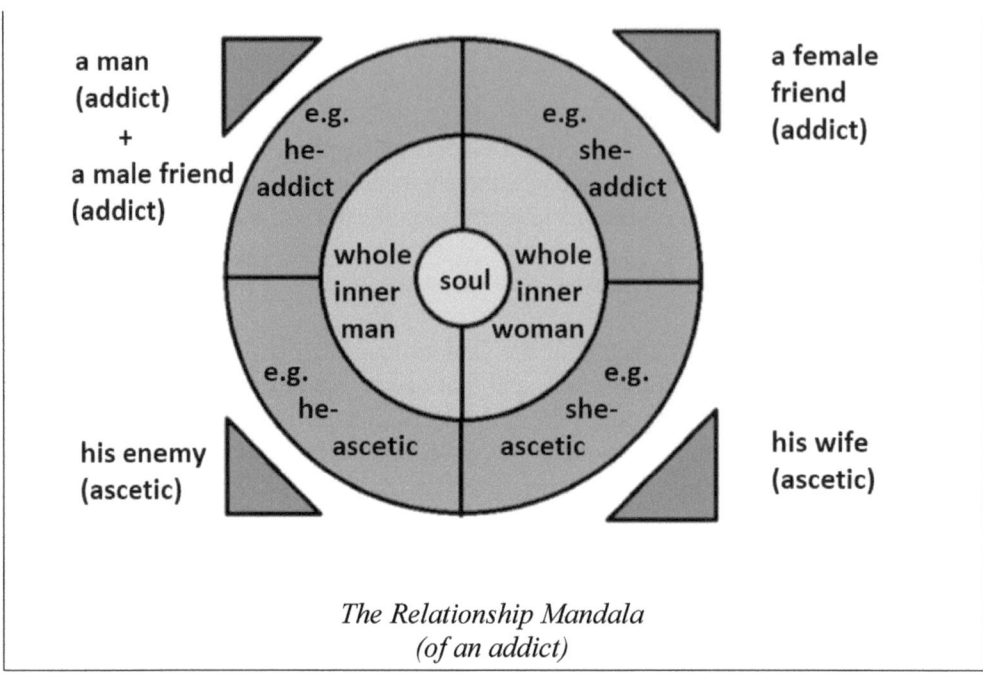

a man
(addict)
+
a male friend
(addict)

a female
friend
(addict)

e.g.
he-
addict

e.g.
she-
addict

whole
inner
man

soul

whole
inner
woman

e.g.
he-
ascetic

e.g.
she-
ascetic

his enemy
(ascetic)

ascetic

ascetic

his wife
(ascetic)

The Relationship Mandala
(of an addict)

III 15. The Horoscope Mandala

The previous mandalas have all been general. However, there are also individual mandalas that look different for each person. The horoscope mandala is one of them. One can use one's own horoscope as the outer area of a mandala – making the inner area of this mandala the "director" of this horoscope show.

For this mandala, one places one's own horoscope on the floor (the symbols of the planets on ten sheets of paper), with the Ascendant (sunrise point) facing east. Then one stands in the center of this mandala and traces the quality that is in the center.

The horoscope is constructed like a play:

    - The ascendant is the stage set,
    - the planets are the actors,
    - the zodiac signs are the roles of these actors,
    - the houses are the areas on the stage (areas of life),
    - the aspects are the script,
    - the ego is the director, and
    - the soul is the scriptwriter.

The horoscope mandala can also be seen as a kind of "internal family constellation".

In the graphic below, the planets have been inserted arbitrarily, since they are in a different place for each person.

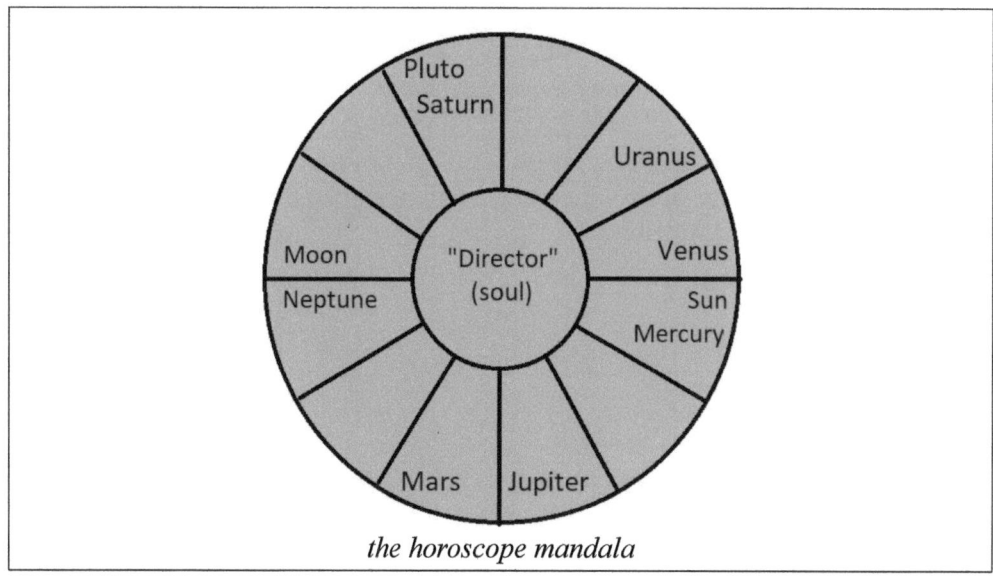

the horoscope mandala

III 16. The individual mandala

One can use the simple Tree of Life Mandala to create a personal mandala containing five elements: one's own body, the three allies (power animal, power plant, power stone), the soul, the guardian deity and God.

Since this mandala does not contain any structures within the circular rings (except for the three allies), this is a path mandala like the labyrinth in Chartre Cathedral – but not the general path, but the personal path to unity.

The following mandala contains examples of these beings – thus it is more vivid.

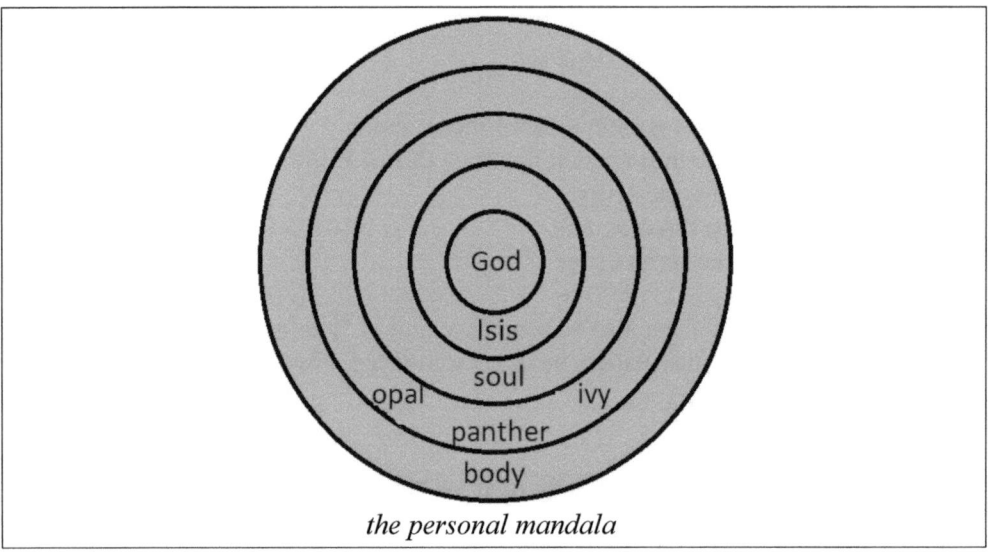

the personal mandala

One can also represent these five levels of beings as a totem pole, in which they are represented one above the other – then this totem pole, like this mandala, would be a symbol of the individual way inward.

III 17.   A Mandala with a Complex Structure

On the Tree of Life, there is an inner structure that becomes visible when the Tree of Life is applied to meditation or to physics. This structure consists of three types of polarity – the thorough description of which, however, is beyond the scope of this book and is given here only to describe the possible mandala structures.

The Polarities on the Tree of Life				
Area	*Sephiroth*	*Polarity*	*Force*	*Man*
center	Kether	1	gravity (one pole: always the same)	God
inner circle	Chokmah, Binah, Da'ath	2	electromagnetic force (two poles: + and -)	protective deity and its opposite pole
middle ring	Chesed, Geburah, Tiphareth	3	color force (three poles: "red", "yellow" and "blue")	soul and its two companions
outer ring	Netzach, Hod, Yesod	2	electromagnetic force (two poles: + and -)	inner man and inner woman
outer border ring	Malkuth	1	gravity (one pole: always the same)	body

From this polarity, similar to the relationship mandala, an all-general mandala with a complex structuring results, which, however, is clearly different from the structure of the relationship mandala.

It is obviously important when designing a mandala to pay close attention to the structures of the area for which you want to design a mandala.

The mandala on the following page is again the Mandala of the Tree of Life – but now a more complete version with the polarieties of the five areas inscibred.

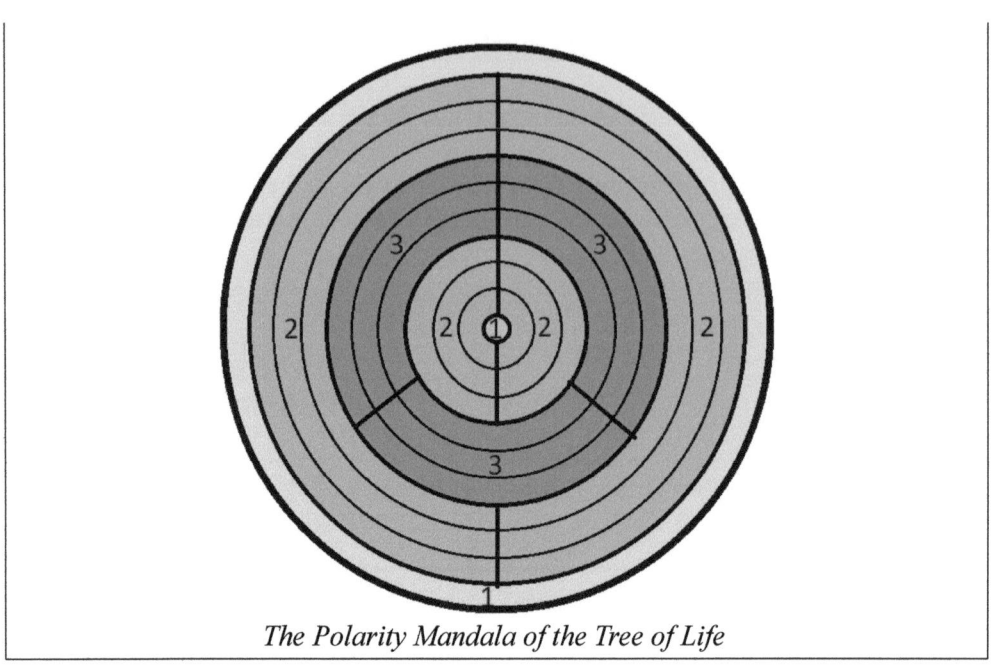

The Polarity Mandala of the Tree of Life

III 18. Deity mandalas

There are especially in Buddhism and with the Indians in the south of the USA and partly also in Hinduism mandalas which belong to a certain deity like in Buddhism to Hevajra, Vajradhara, Dakini etc. or with the Navaho-Indians to Changing Woman. These mandalas have an individual structure that reflects the character of the deity in question and its effect on man. These mandalas can usually only be understood if one has a great deal of prior knowledge about the deity in question.

III 19. New Mandalas

There are the traditional mandalas like those of the Tibetans and the Navaho Indians as well as the mandalas that can be derived from already known structures like the Tree of Life. But one can also discover completely new Mandalas at any time such as the Relationship Mandala.

Therefore, one can always design a mandala for the area in which one is particularly interested, once one has recognized the inner structure of the area in question.

III 20. The "I Ching" Mandala

The Chinese book "I Ching" ("Book of Changes") is based on ancient Chinese mythology:

- In the beginning was the Tao, the unity behind all appearance.

- The Tao divided into the Yin (otherworld) and the Yang (this world).

- Yin and Yang combined with each other to form the 4 basic elements ("digrams"), which correspond to the four seasons of the day and the four seasons of the year.

- These 4 basic elements divided again into the 8 trigrams, which are the basic states in the world.

- The 64 possible transformations of these 8 trigrams into another one of the 8 trigrams (or into the same trigram) result in the 64 hexagrams of the I Ching, on which the "I Ching" oracle is based.

From these 8·8 transformation possibilities, among other things, the game board was created, which is used in chess, checkers and Go and consists of 8·8 fields.

The traditional derivation of the 64 hexagrams of the I Ching is shown in the following table. The assignment of the times of the day and the seasons to the four digrams was added by me, but it results from the inner logic of the symbolism of the I Ching.

The hexagrams of the I Ching				
Unity	*Yin/Yang*	*Digrams*	*Trigrams*	*Hexagrams*
point	*1 line*	*2 lines*	*3 lines*	*6 lines*
o Tao	--- Heaven	-- young Yang, --- morning, spring	--- -- fire ---	eight combinations of "fire" and another trigram
			-- -- thunder ---	eight combinations of "thunder" and another trigram
		--- old Yang, --- day, summer	--- --- sky ---	eight combinations of "sky" and another trigram
			-- --- lake ---	eight combinations of "lake" and another trigram
	-- Earth	--- young Yin, -- evening, harvest	--- --- wind --	eight combinations of "wind" and another trigram
			-- --- water --	eight combinations of "water" and another trigram
		-- old Yin, -- night, winter	--- -- mountain --	eight combinations of "mountain" and another trigram
			-- -- Earth --	eight combinations of "earth" and another trigram

As a mandala, this rather static structure, in which life, however, constantly flows from one place to another, looks like the following graphic. In this mandala opposites are always found exactly in opposition like "heaven" and "earth" or "fire" and "water".

The 64 hexagrams in the outer circle have been inserted in the following mandala graphic only as small boxes, but without their names.

One could argue, that this is not a mandala but a differentiation system. But as the way from the hexagrams on the outside to the Tao in the center is also a way to the essence, this is a "classical mandala" – but a quite unusual one.

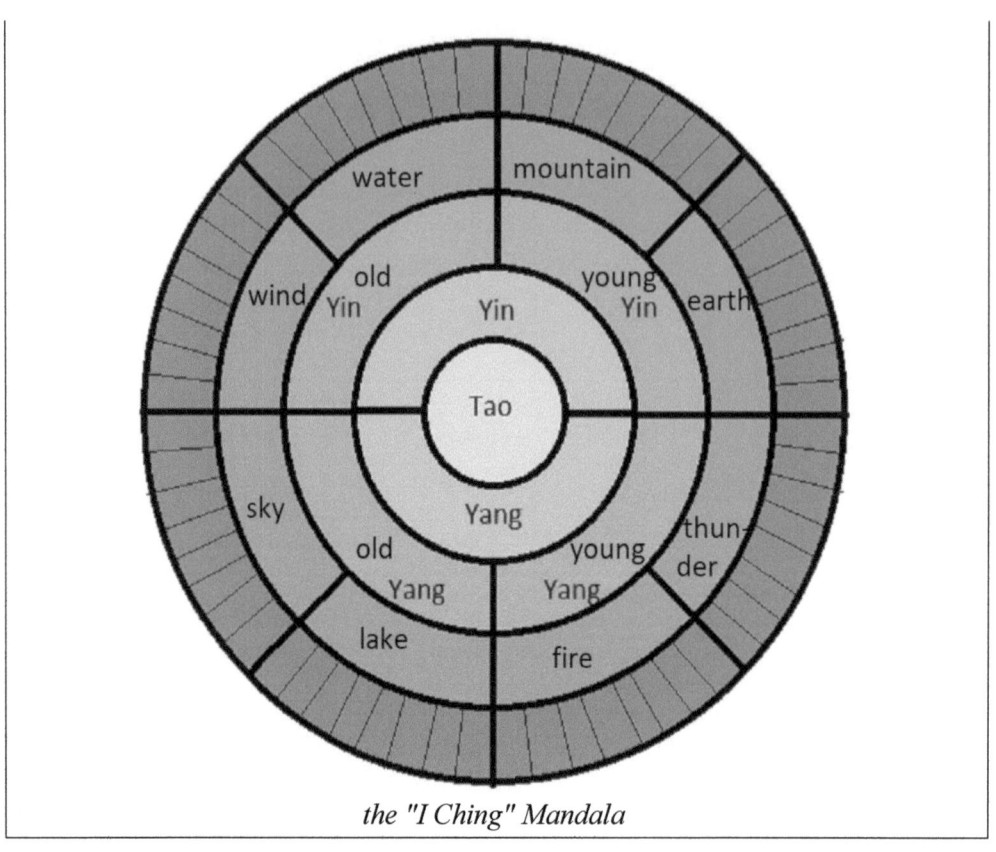

the "I Ching" Mandala

A very similar mandala could be designed for the West African Ifa oracle, which is constructed quite similarly to the I Ching. It consists of 16·16=256 qualities instead of the 8·8=64 qualities of the I Ging.

III 21. The "Flower of Life"

This mandala is a "continuum mandala", so to speak, since it has no center and can be extended arbitrarily in any direction. Therefore, the "Flower of Life" is more of an endless pattern or symbol than a mandala. It represents the 60° angle, which in astrology represents the "community of similar elements".

Similar endless mandalas can also be made, for example, with hexagrams (honeycombs), triangles and squares. However, they have no inner structure, but are the "homogeneous representation" of the quality of a certain angle or possibly of other geometric shapes. For this reason the "Flower of Life" is no mandala.

The "Flower of Life" is constructed by drawing a circle and then a second circle of the same size, whose center is on the first circle. If you then draw more circles with the same radius, whose center is always on the intersections of at least two circles, the result is the "Flower of Life".

"Flower of Life"

49

III 22.   An Oracle Mandala

One possible use of a mandala is the "bone oracle". Here one uses one or two dozen of small objects, which one has found in the course of time in "conspicuous situations". This can be a tooth as a symbol for "strength", a bone for "constancy", an acorn for "essence", a rock crystal for "clarity", a feather for "lightness", a gold nugget for "soul", a stone with an eye-like grain for "attention", a coin for "prosperity", and so on.

Of these items, which can be kept in a bag, for example, you take out a handful at random and let them roll over a piece of cloth on which you have painted a mandala. This can be, for example, the mandala with the four elements and the quintessence in their center. The position of the objects on the mandala then gives the answer to the question asked.

If, for example, the feather is placed on the field "fire", it is easy for the person to use his power. If the eye-like stone lies on the earth field, one concentrates mainly on everyday things like e.g. earning money.

For such an oracle, one should use a mandala whose symbolism is quite familiar to oneself.

III 23.   Symbols an Deities

Many mandalas contain symbols that identify and describe the individual areas of the mandalas. Since these symbols often come from other cultures, it is often necessary to explore this symbolic language if one wants to understand the mandala.

In a lot of cases these symbols are deities – thes inhabit the mandala-city.

IV   The Creation of a Mandala

The construction of a mandala takes place in several phases, all of which have different functions.

IV 1.   The Choice of the Mandala

The first step is the choice of the mandala, which depends on the goal of the person or group who wants to create a mandala.

In addition to the goal, it also depends, of course, on the culture of the people in question: Tibetans will make a sand image in a monastery, Navahos will make a sand image in a sacred place, and in the megalithic culture standing stones would have been erected.

It also depends on the choice of style, i.e. culture, in which way the mandala is made: from colored sand, from stones, perhaps only from images placed on the ground, or from a circle of statuettes.

The statues of the saints on the two quarter-circle arches in St. Peter's Square in Rome with the obelisk in the center are also a mandala – albeit a mandala made in a very elaborate way.

IV 2.   Drawing the Mandala

Next, the mandala is sketched – unless it has a traditional shape that is used every time.

Then the outline of the mandala is drawn on the earth, on the floor in the temple, etc. Since mandalas are usually very symmetrical, this ground plan drawing consists mainly of concentric circles, squares, diagonals and the like. It is advisable to be very careful when drawing the ground plan, otherwise the mandala will be crooked and you may have to start all over again – of course, this is especially true for the large and complex mandalas, e.g. the mandalas from Tibet.

IV 3.   Coloring the Mandala

If a pictorial mandala is to be made, now follows the coloring of the sketch. The pictures in the mandala are usually arranged symmetrically like the forms of the mandala: E.g. in the outer ring in each of the four directions the animal that belongs to this direction – in a North American sweat lodge ritual thus the snake in the west, the bear in the north, the eagle in the east and the buffalo in the south. In an occidental mandala, these could be the four archangels: Raphael in the east, Michael in the south, Gabriel in the west, and Auriel in the north.

In terms of the physical production of the mandala, this is the most elaborate phase. For example, if the mandala is made of colored sand, as is customary in Tibet, and is 3 meters in diameter, this represents many days of work, in which the geometric surfaces are sprinkled with colored sand and then filled with ornaments and deity figures made of colored sand.

There are, of course, much simpler mandalas such as a circle of ten sheets of paper on which the symbols of the ten planets have been painted and which are laid out in the circle so that they correspond to the position of the planets in the horoscope of the person for whom this "astrological mandala" is being created.

The most elaborate mandalas of all are the temples constructed as mandalas.

IV 4.   Understanding the Mandala

An important point that should be considered at this point at the latest is the under-standing of the mandala by those who want to participate in the mandala ritual. The mandala works even if you don't understand it, but in general the effect should be greater if you understand what you are doing and why.

However, as with almost everything, understanding does not replace doing.

IV 5.   The First Imagination of the Mandala

When the mandala has been completed, the next step is to look at it and then imagine it internally with closed eyes. It will be advisable for most people to first imagine the rough structure of the mandala internally (How many concentric circles? How many directions?), then the medium structures (What beings are depicted in the mandala?), and finally the subtleties (What are the colors of the ornaments on the city gates?).

It is important that the mandala becomes an inner image. It should become so vivid that you can walk around in it internally – similar to how you can clearly imagine the way to the next supermarket internally with your eyes closed.

There are also mandalas that are only imagined and have no external form. The best known mandala of this kind in the western culture will probably be the "Lesser Pentagram Ritual". It consists of a circle, a pentagram in each of the four directions corresponding to the four elements, an archangel in each of the four directions, and a hexagram above the center, i.e., if you look at the mandala two-dimensionally, in the center.

Another very simple mandala from the Golden Dawn tradition is the "Journey to the Temple of the Sun". This mandala has already been described: One walks through a desert in one's meditation, enters a city, and then goes to the temple in the center of that city, where one calls one's soul and one's power animal.

Imagining a mandala requires frequent repetition and practice – it will usually take a while before the images really come to life before your inner eye and you encounter unexpectedly, for example, people in the imagined mandala city who greet you in a friendly manner.

IV 6.   Filling the Mandala with the Elements of the World

This step serves to make the universal meaning of the mandala come alive in one-self. One looks at all the things one encounters in everyday life to see where they belong in the mandala. If you use a very simple mandala, which consists only of the circle of the four elements and the quintessence in the middle, you ask yourself, for example, with all things, to which element they belong.

With such a simple mandala, of course, you have to look at what is the main aspect of a thing. For example, a stove belongs primarily to fire, a bathtub to water, a vacuum cleaner to air, the bed to earth, and the house altar to light, that is, to the quintessence.

IV 7.   Filling the Mandala with the Elements of One's Own Psyche

Next, this mapping is also done with one's own inner elements. For example, courage belongs to fire, love to water, truth to air, thriving to earth and identity to light. One can also assign individual experiences and feelings to the mandala.

By this assignment the mandala gets meaning and finally becomes alive – and one establishes a personal bond to this mandala.

The stronger the mandala is anchored in the outside and in the inside, the more power and depth the images this mandala will evolve – and the greater will be the effect of the rituals one performs with this mandala.

However, there follow other methods by which the mandala also comes alive.

IV 8.   The Second Imagination of the Mandala

When the individual parts of the simple or complex mandala have received a deeper meaning and an anchoring in the outside and in the inside by the assignments, the imagination of the mandala will become simpler and more lively and will receive increasingly more details.

Possibly now also the effect occurs that one not only imagines inner pictures, but that during the imagining things appear to one that one has not imagined – a detail, a color, a person on the streets of the imagined city, a tree, etc. These perceptions and images should be included in the mandala if they are in harmony with its structure, which will usually be the case.

When such images have appeared a few times "out of the mandala", one will get a different feeling about the mandala: It begins to come alive and take on a momentum of its own – it becomes alive.

Walking the paths through the mandala then gradually becomes as "real" and full of unpredictable things as the way to the next post office, where you also do not know beforehand whom you might meet.

IV 9. The Dream Journeys into the Mandala

The next step consists of the dream journeys to the individual aspects of the mandala.

For example, if you want to learn how to lead a sweat lodge, it makes a lot of sense to take a few days, possibly fast, and do a dream journey to one aspect of the sweat lodge mandala each day: to the serpent Sintela in the west, to the great bear Mahto in the north, to the eagle Wambli in the east, to the white buffalo woman Pte-san-win in the south, to grandfather sun Tunka-shila in the sky above, to grandmother earth Unki Maka below, and to the great mystery Wakan Tanka in the center.

The sweat lodge mandala is three-dimensional – in ancient cultures, as here, there are usually seven directions: the four cardinal points, the top, the bottom and the center.

These dream journeys can be done in different details – once in each direction or to each detail of the mandala.

By the encounters one will have on these dream journeys, by the conversations one will have with the beings there, or by the gifts one will receive from them, by the advice or the healings one can find there – by all of this the mandala will once again change fundamentally: It will grow from being a concept to something alive, which one will naturally use in everyday life.

When you have experienced that the Serpent knows how to awaken the Kundalini, that the Great Bear can help you to become steadfast and resistant to stress, that the Eagle can find new ways, that the White Buffalo Woman can dissolve loneliness, that Grandfather Sun knows how to bear responsibility, that Grandmother Earth can restore your confidence, and that the Great Mystery can make you more alive – then, when you have a problem, you will turn to them for advice and help without thinking twice.

When one has made such dream journeys, one will receive contact with the beings of the mandala, with the archangels, with the deities, with the Buddhas, with the animals, etc. – and this will become a living contact that will make one's life easier.

This is an important step in building a mandala – only by these dream journeys does the mandala really come alive.

IV 10.   The way into the mandala

The way into the mandala is the most important element of the mandala – after all, the mandala is a map of the "inside of the world", which serves to reach the center of the world – the "heart of life".

The simplest mandalas consist only of this path: a spiral in which one can go from the outside to the inside. The spirals that go clockwise inward are concentrating; the spirals that go clockwise outward are creating. This inward and backward path is the path the shaman takes in the otherworld journey.

This spiral otherworld journey is still carried out today, especially in Waldorf kindergartens during Advent, as an "Advent garden". Here the spiral is laid out on the floor with fir branches and tealights – the children then go individually to the singing of the other children into this spiral to the center (from where they can take, for example, an apple) and then go out again.

A more complex variant of the otherworld spiral is the labyrinth. Originally, this was a single path like the spiral, but in the labyrinth it winds back and forth on its way to the center. This form of labyrinth dates back to the Neolithic period and can be found, for example, on the floor of Chartre Cathedral.

The labyrinths with branches leading astray are a more recent version, intended to illustrate the difficulty of getting to the otherworld and back again.

In most mandalas, however, there are four paths that lead straight from the edge of the mandala to the center of the mandala. They are also otherworld paths – four variations corresponding to the four qualities of the four directions. Originally, however, these four-part mandalas will have been understood differently, since the four directions represent the phases of the sun's course:

The Four Directions			
Direction	*Sun*	*Man*	*Way*
east	Sunrise	birth	the way from the otherworld to this world
south	Day	life	the way in this world
west	sunset	death	the way from this world to the otherworld
north	night	Tod	the way in the otherworld

From this representation of the cycle then gradually the fourfold way to the center developed, which was connected among other things with the four elements. The dynamic circle became the static cross-circle. This cross-circle (⊗) is a symbol of the sun in many cultures – the sun being the symbol of both the circular cycle and the

56

center.

In the mandala dream journey one goes now these ways from the border to the center (and possibly also real in the temple) and looks, what one experiences on them. The experiences will probably be rather inconspicuous in the beginning, but they will gain intensity in the course of time.

IV 11.   The Guardians of the City Gates

An interesting phenomenon are the "guardians of the city gates". When the mandala is conceived and imagined as a city, there are gates between each of the circular rings on the four paths from the edge to the center. These gates correspond to different aspects of the world or of the human being.

Using a mandala of one circle and four rings divided into the four directions, there are five gates on each of the four paths – making a total of twenty gates.

1. the four gates to the outer border-ring: *the entrance*

The guards in these four gates are quite harmless, as they only require the determination to focus on the mandala, since the outer border-ring is the material world and one's own body.

2. the four gates to the outer ring: *the threshold*

The outer ring is the psyche. In order to enter it, one needs to concentrate, then to look inward, and thirdly, to be willing to look at the unknown or unloved in oneself and in the world. If one carries great addictions or fears or self-doubts within oneself, it could be that one already experiences some of these at these gates – then the guards at these gates would already be a bit more unpleasant.

3. the four gates to the middle ring: *the trench*

The third ring seen from the outside is the realm of the soul. Therefore, if one wants to enter this area, it can happen that one encounters the part of one's own psyche that C.G. Jung calls the "shadow", that is, the repressed part of one's own psyche. Possibly

57

one also encounters here the aspects of the world that one fears.

Consequently, one can encounter at these gates the things that are normally difficult for one's own perception because one fears them. These aspects of one's being or of the world can be encountered at the four gates leading into the circular ring of the soul – but this does not necessarily have to happen.

If one uses a mandala divided into the four elements, the guardians at the gates to the circular ring of the soul might take the following forms, for example:

> - If one tends to repress one's aggressions, one could meet an "aggressive monster" at the gate to the ring of the soul – probably on the path of fire in the south, if one uses an element mandala.

> - In the east on the air path, at the threshold to the soul, one could meet the "spirit of lies" that leads one astray – if one is often afraid to tell the truth.

> - If one is tormented by fears of abandonment, one could meet the "lonely child" at the threshold to the soul in the west on the Water Way.

> - On the earth path in the north one could possibly meet the "hunger suffe-rer" at the threshold of the gate to the soul, if one is often tormented by exis-tential fears.

4. the four gates to the inner ring: *the abyss*

The innermost circular ring is the area of the deities in the mandala considered here. Since a deity has a clearly contoured quality, but is without boundaries ("infinite"), one is confronted with the letting go of all boundaries at these four gates. This can possibly be experienced as a leap into a bottomless abyss or as walking along a forest path that suddenly dissolves into the darkness between the stars.

This realm corresponds to the four boundless qualities that, according to Buddha, characterize an enlightened being: boundless equanimity, boundless compassion, boundless love, and boundless joy. If one can let go of everything with joy, this transition is no problem – but if one is still holding on to or keeping anything away, this transition can become difficult. Then one experiences these four boundless qua-lities as what in Tibetan Buddhism is called the "raging and blood-drinking deities".

If one is not able to welcome everything that exists in the world (the innermost ring), then when one crosses the threshold to this ring, one will be confronted with the things that one does not want to have – this may become violent.

For this reason, it is always recommended to take the path into the inner world step by step and not just rush off. On the other hand, it is not a catastrophe if you have such a frightening experience at this threshold – you then know what to expect and you can prepare for it by making friends with what you have feared and by letting go of what you have clinged to.

This may sound a bit destructive or self-torturing, but that is not what is meant here – on the contrary, approaching this transition is a very thorough form of healing. This consists of seeing the world and oneself as they are – and then looking at what one does. One stops closing one's eyes to reality – and then, with a greater contact with reality, can better achieve (and possibly transform) one's goals.

If one approaches these four gates to the ring of deities and is very thorough in doing so, the world gradually becomes transparent: one can see everything wherever one looks. This includes distant places as well as the past and the future. Just before these four gates, one enters the archive of the world, so to speak. This also means that here you can see all your previous incarnations – and, if you want, also your own future including your own death. However, this only happens if one really performs the meditations, dream journeys and rituals of this mandala very thoroughly.

This "transparency" is the preliminary stage to the "dissolution of boundaries" when jumping into the bottomless abyss.

5. the four gates to the central circle: *the dissolution of form*

In the transition to unity, one can have experiences that are quite far out of the ordinary. They are all the return to oneness and therefore dissolve all distinction.

The center is simply glistening white light.

- - -

These five transitions at the entrance and at the four gates on each of the four wafs to the centre have been described here with the more intense experiences – simply to describe the possible depth of experiences in a mandala.

However, the intensity of the experiences in a mandala depends on many things: on one's own motivation, on the intensity of the imaginations, on one's own character (temperament, horoscope), on one's own biography (repressed fears and addictions, traumas), the previous magical-spiritual experiences, the people with whom one possibly performs the mandala meditations and mandala rituals together, etc.

Sometimes it happens that one reaches very far in the direction of the center and has e.g. a vision of one's own soul, but then a longer lean spell is encountered, in which one must first integrate again what one has experienced and simply has to continue to practice.

But it can also happen that one simply has new experiences in small bites and there is no dramatic dynamic.

Sometimes one can get quite far without consciously dealing with the guardians of the gates and only meets them later … there are many ways in which this "journey to the center" can take place.

IV 12. The Areas inside the Rings

In the example of a mandala used here, which consists of four rings and a center, it can happen that on the way through one of the rings, one notices that it is subdivided once again, whereby these sub-areas are only separated from each other by smaller gates, thresholds, steps and the like.

These sub-areas correspond, among others, to the Sephirah from the Kabbalistic Tree of Life:

outer border-ring: body

outer ring: psyche
- *one's own life force*: Here one can meet one's own power animal, one's own power plant and one's own power stone.
- *one's own thinking*: Here one can possibly find more clarity.
- *one's own feeling*: Here one can find new strength and joy of life.

middle ring: soul
- *one's own soul*: Here one can meet one's own soul, i.e. exactly that part of one's own soul which has currently incarnated in oneself. As long as one has not recognized one's own soul as one's own center, it appears to one in the outside as a "guardian spirit" or "guardian angel".
- *one's own karma*: Here one can encounter the reasons that have led to one's current incarnation.
- *one's own incarnations*: Here one can encounter the circle of one's own previous incarnations, as well as the "light" that has incarnated in all these people one once lived as. Here is the "archive of one's incarnations", where, if one wishes, one can also look at the rest of one's life as one's soul has planned and created it.

inner circle ring: deities
- *one's own protective deity*: here one can meet the deity of which one's own soul is a part – the soul is, so to speak, a drop from the sea

of this deity. Therefore, this deity is one's own "protective deity".
- *the community*: Here one can experience oneself or one's own deity as a part of the whole – as a cell of a large organism.
- *the light storm*: Here one experiences one's own essence and thus also the essence of one's guardian deity in its completely unhindered expansion and in its completely unhindered self-expression.

inner circle: God

This further differentiation is meant to illustrate two things above all: First, the possible richness of inner experiences one can have in a mandala, and second, the way in which a mandala can become more and more differentiated by one's own experiences.

This differentiation, especially of the rings of the mandala, can be most vividly illustrated by an overview:

The progressive differentiation of a mandala				
1. step	*2. step*	*3. step*	*4. step*	*Tree of life*
life	God	God	God	Kether
	way	deities	light storm	Chokmah
			community	Binah
			protective deity	Da'ath
		soul	soul archive	Chesed
			karma	Geburah
			soul	Tiphareth
		psyche	feeling	Netzach
			thinking	Hod
			life force	Yesod
	world/body	world/body	world/body	Malkuth

On the Tree of Life there are also all the gates of the mandala (apart from the "entrance") are found:

- The gate between the body ring and the psyche ring is called "threshold".

- The gate between the psyche ring and the soul ring is called "trench".

- The gate between the soul ring and the deity ring is called "abyss".

- The gate between the deity ring and the unitiy-circle could be called "last step" (or also "forst step").

These considerations show, among other things, that when you use a mandala, you should also make sure that you use correct degrees of differentiation. So in the beginning it will be useful to use only one circle and four circular rings, otherwise the meditator could be confused. The differentiation of the three inner circular rings into three further sub-areas each can be added later, when one has already become familiar with the mandala.

Furthermore, it shows that a mandala, which is a concentric structure, can still have the same basic message as, for example, the Tree of Life, since both represent a path. The basic idea is the same for both: the way from the outside to the inside. This path is also found in yoga as the sequence of the different forms of yoga from hatha yoga to raja yoga, in Buddhism as the step path ("lamrim"), in Sufism as the rose path, and so on.

IV 13. The Invocation of the Mandala Deities

A mandala can be seen in two ways:

- on the one hand as the path from one's own body (outside) to God (inside): one's own "path of enlightenment";

- on the other hand, as different ways of looking at the world: from multiplicity outside to unity inside.

In the first case the wandering in the mandala shows above all the own development and the own "umbilical cord to God", thus what "religion" actually means: "reconnection" ("re-ligio"). In this case, the deities are found only in the innermost ring of the circle – only there one meets them on one's own journey to the center.

In the second case, the mandala shows the different areas of the world and the different ways in which it can be viewed. In this case the whole mandala is an archetype of the world, which is why deities can be found in all areas – in the ring of the psyche e.g. the deities of the life force (Isis, Freya, Pte-san-win etc.), the deities of the mind (Thot, Hermes, Mercury etc.) and the deities of the feelings (Aphrodite, Venus, Lofn etc.). Deities are also found at the gates as guardians of the threshold (Janus, Loki, Devil, etc.).

No matter which of the two possible versions of a mandala one uses, it is useful to make dream journeys to the deities in the mandala after a while. You should ask the deities what they want to tell you or show you, what is important for you to discover, or if they want to add something to the mandala.

The most intensive form of contact with a deity is the invocation. Such an invocation is a "calling in" ("in-vocare") of a deity into oneself. There are two basic variants for this:

> Ritual: One stands in the room and imagines the deity in front of oneself at a distance of a few meters.
> > - Then one begins to describe it: "She is ..."
> > - Next, one addresses the deity directly and feels it: "You are ..."
> > - Then you move towards it or call it to you and unite its shape with your own: "I am ...".
> > - Possibly this is followed by an action that one performs as this deity, i.e. a healing, a wish or the like: "I do ..."

> Dream journey: In this variant, one undertakes a dream journey to the deity and then sees it internally. The dream journey takes the place of the description and the addressing of the deity in the previous method. Then one asks the deity whether one may cross over into it with one's own consciousness. If so, one does so.

Such invocations can also have a very different intensity. This can range from a vague feeling for the deity, to intense feelings, to the vision of the deity in the room in front of you.

The essential point is ultimately the question of what this deity can show you, what part of yourself it can heal and how it can enrich your life and make it happier. This is of course again very different for everyone ...

You can also assign the levels of invocation to the rings and the central circle of the mandala. This list is read from the bottom to the top:

The levels of invocation in the mandala			
Mandala	*Man*	*Contact*	*Invocation*
central circle	god	-	-
inner ring	deity	action	„I do ...“
middle ring	soul	identity	„I am ...“
outer ring	psyche	opposition	„You are ...“
border ring	body	contemplation	„She is ...“

IV 14. The Third Imagination of the Mandala

By the various contemplations, imaginations, dream journeys and invocations, the mandala has become more complex and vivid. By this time the imagination of the mandala will probably have become quite independent and stable, i.e. the inner images will begin to be colorful, to glow from within, independently acting beings will appear in the mandala, one will receive advice and help from them, etc.

At this point at the latest, the mandala becomes an "everyday tool": When one needs advice and help with a particular issue, one will turn to the mandala, i.e. to a particular being in the mandala, and ask them for help – what works, one does simply because it works. For example, if one is short of money, one will go to the earth path in the mandala and ask one of the beings there for assistance – which will come.

Also the stages in which the imaginations develop can be assigned to the rings of the mandala. In the following overview also the transitions between the rings (the gates, if one has imagined the mandala as a city) are listed, because there are sometimes quite striking perceptions at them.

Theway from the outside to inside again leads from the bottom of the list to the top of the list.

The types of imagination and vision in the mandala		
Mandala	*Man*	*Perception*
central circle	God	glistening white light
first (last) step		*Tor zum Licht*
inner ring	deities	brightly shining figures in bright light
abyss		*letting go*
middle ring	soul	symbols shining from inside, still images, hardly any movements
trench		*glow from inside, extremely sharp contours, constantly changing shapes*
outer ring	psyche	colorless shadow, diffuse light source
threshold		*concentration*
border ring	body	image outside

IV 15. The Mandala Ritual

The ritual of the mandala depends to a great extent on the theme of the mandala. For example, if it shows in the four cardinal points the grain god, the earth goddess, the rain god, and the wind god, then the mandala is obviously used for increasing crop yields. The ritual associated with this mandala is then a fertility spell.

A mandala with the four winds is obviously used for wind spells and possibly also for rain spells.

The relationship mandala, on the other hand, is very personal and is used to make one's relationships more pleasant by healing one's inner male image and one's inner female image. The ritual here results from healing these two inner images.

From the typical mandala, which represents the path from outside to inside, from multiplicity to unity, arise path rituals and transition rituals. These are the great number of initiation rituals, of which the ceremonies of the Golden Dawn are probably the best known at present. However, there are such rites of passage in almost every magical order, in every witchcraft circle, in every Masonic lodge and among many primitive peoples.

Here everyone must look for himself whether he finds rituals or groups whose style suits him. All in all no complex, formal rituals are necessary, but they can certainly have a great effect – if they are either performed alone with great intensity or if they are led by people who themselves have had many magical-spiritual experiences. If one finds such experienced people, cooperation with them can definitely be a great help.

But it is also possible to walk the path to the center without rituals – then the experiences on the dream journeys take over the function that otherwise the rituals have: one's own healing and transformation.

If one has experience with family constellations, one can mark the mandala with colored threads or similar on the floor and then bodily walk from the outside to the inside and each time talk to the place in the mandala, feel into the quality of that aspect of the mandala, etc.

The important point is that you should start – but only with a mandala that expresses an essential concern of yours, otherwise you will lack the true, intense motivation that should eventually be the basis of all action. When you have started to design the mandala, to paint it or something similar and then you have carried out the first imaginations and dream journeys, a dynamic will arise by itself that will lead you further in the direction of the center of the mandala.

Possibly even a figure appears in the dream journeys, which leads one through the mandala …

IV 16.   The transformations at the gates

The gates are the transitions on the way to the center, when one wants to get from one ring to the next ring. These are the actual, important steps on this path. At these gates you integrate something, you let go of something, you heal something, you are courageous, etc. This means that at these gates the actual transformations take place.

There one can meet the guardians of the threshold who embody one's own fears, addictions and doubts – here there is a great variety of possible images that can appear at these gates as monsters. Approaching these monsters, contacting them, getting to know them is what ultimately brings healing.

What is needed to transform such a monster, such an image of fear or addiction, into something else is quite simple: look, feel, embrace.

> - By stopping and looking at the monster, you begin to understand what appears to you as a monster, you understand where it comes from, what it wants, what character it has.

> - By turning to the monster and by feeling what it is, one connects to it, one

understands its interior and thus one's own interior and recognizes its essence and its inner need.

- By opening oneself and embracing the monster, one takes the monster back into oneself and can thereby consciously integrates it.

The real problem is not the experiences during this integration, but the fear of the monster itself – the "fear of fear". This is one of the processes that are difficult to explain in words – you have to try it out and experience it.

It may be possible to use a family constellation at this point, by which the monster and the theme connected with it become clearer. Thereby one can understand the monster better and possibly already heal it.

At the gates also new abilities are acquired, which correspond to the ring area, which one wants to enter:

- the gate to the body ring: the ability to be present in the here and now

- the gate between the body ring and the psyche ring: the dream journey and the life force in general

- the gate between the psyche ring and the soul ring: the inner silence (only the consciousness that is aware of itself)

- the gate between the soul ring and the deity ring: the letting go of any delimitation and the resting of one's own individuality in one's own quality

- the gate between the deity ring and the God-circle: the letting go of any separation.

IV 17. The Transformations in the Rings

Transformations also take place in the circle rings themselves, but they have a completely different character than the transformations at the gates between the rings.

In a mandala, whose four sides correspond to the four elements, one goes to the center on four different paths during different dream journeys. Thereby one experiences the four elements on different levels (rings):

- body ring: concrete earth, water, air and fire

- psyche: the fire of power, the water of love, the air of truth and the earth of prosperity

- soul ring: the fire of transformation, the water of connectedness, the air of movement, the earth of permanence

- deity ring: Raphael, the archangel of the air; Michael, the archangel of the fire; Gabriel, the archangel of the water; and Auriel, the archangel of the earth

- God circle: Unity

In each of the four rings there is a division into four quarters corresponding to the four elements. In each of these rings, it is useful and helpful to look at the relationships between these four areas.

In the area of the body, for example, one can look at where fire affects earth (forging), where fire affects water (cooking), where water affects earth (watering flowers), and so on.

Such observations can be made in each of the four circular rings.

The four paths do not exist separately from each other, but are aspects of the same path from outside to inside.

Of these four paths, one will usually first choose the one one is most familiar with – Aries, Leo and Sagittarius tend to choose the Fire path; Cancer, Scorpio and Pisces the Water path; Libra, Aquarius and Gemini the Air path; and Capricorn, Taurus and Virgo the Earth path.

It is necessary, however, to supplement the preferred path with the other three paths in order to dissolve one's own one-sidedness. Often one finds the greatest treasures on the path one dislikes the most – that which one dislikes is something repressed that longs for re-integration …

IV 18.   The union of the paths

When one has arrived at the innermost ring of the mandala and wants to enter the circle in the center, one must unite the four paths – how else can unity be achieved in the center?

For this, first of all, it is necessary that one has recognized the characteristics of the four ways by contemplations, dream journeys, invocations, and so on.

Next, it is necessary to recognize these four qualities as colors in a continuum, as sounds in a melody, as phases of a transformation. For this it is conducive to transform these four qualities into each other in one's own imagination: Fire becomes water, fire becomes air, fire becomes earth, water becomes fire, water becomes earth, water becomes air, etc.

This transformation contemplation can be done in three ways:

1. the state of matter transformations:
   - Solid (earth) becomes liquid (water): melting
   - Liquid (water) becomes gaseous (air): boiling
   - Gaseous (air) becomes plasma (fire): atomic bomb
   - Plasma (fire) becomes gaseous (air): nuclear fusion
   - Gaseous (air) becomes liquid (water): condensation
   - Liquid (water) becomes solid (earth): freezing

There are also transitions e.g. from solid to gaseous (sublimation), but the transitions in the sequence "solid – liquid – gaseous – plasma" are the important transitions.

2. the element transformations:
   - Fire becomes air: the smoke over the fire
   - Fire becomes water: thunderstorm
   - Fire becomes earth: ashes
   - Water becomes fire: burning oil
   - Water becomes air: steam, fog, clouds
   - Water becomes earth: ice
   - Air becomes fire: burning gas
   - Air becomes water: dew
   - Air becomes earth: hoarfrost
   - Earth becomes fire: burning coals
   - Earth becomes air: dust
   - Earth becomes water: molten metal

These are just a few simple examples, which should be supplemented with other images to bring these transformations to life.

The important thing is not that the pictures are "physically correct" in all details (after all, the four elements are not a physical concept), but that one gets a feeling for the interaction of the four elements and for their transformations into each other.

3. the quality transformations:
- Strength (fire) helps to speak the truth (air).
- Strength (fire) gives the courage to love (water).
- Strength (fire) enables the achievement of flourishing (earth).
- Truth (air) helps to find one's strength (fire).
- Truth (Air) leads to the expression of love (Water).
- Truth (Air) makes one act successfully and prosper (Earth).
- Love (Water) gives great strength (Fire).
- Love (Water) lets the truth (Air) be known.
- Love (Water) creates life (Earth).
- Thriving (Earth) gives health (Fire).
- Thriving (Earth) helps to realize the effective (Air).
- Thriving (earth) promotes love (water) for life.

These four elements are also what a fortune teller is asked about: "I want to know (air) all about money (earth), love (water) and health (fire)."

These contemplations should not only be done intellectually, but they should also be imagined intensely. It is useful to always imagine the four elements in their direction in the mandala: usually, therefore, fire in the south, air in the east, water in the west and earth in the north. By this directional relationship, the elements remain connected to the mandala during these contemplations and imaginations.

By these contemplations, the boundaries between the four elements dissolve in one's understanding and they become one continuum. This boundary-less state is the prerequisite for moving from the innermost ring to the circle in the center.
This dissolution of boundaries is all the more effective, the better the four elements are anchored as a concept in one's own psyche. To achieve this, contemplations, imaginations, dream journeys and invocations are the best tools. One can always transform in a mandala only what one has put into it – by the various forms of ritual and meditation.
This state of continuum has been described here as a realization and as an imagination, but it can be experienced in a very real way – the realization is only a tool to get to the experience … a door opener, so to speak. The experience of the continuum, which is typical of the ring of deities, is one of the things that can be pointed out, but which can be understood only if one has experienced it oneself.
And this experience is worthwhile!

IV 19.   The Center

The center is the origin, the source, the essence of the mandala. The quality of this center depends, of course, on the mandala being viewed:

> - A mandala with the Earth Goddess, the Grain God, the Rain God and the Wind God in the four directions has as its center the abundant harvest.
>
> - The relationship mandala has as its center one's soul.
>
> - The horoscope mandala also has as its center also one's own soul.
>
> - The mandala of the four rings and the four directions has God as its center.

Not much can be said about the experience of this center … It is an "It is." It is unformed, unstructured, resting in itself, radiant … It is what the Dakota Indians call it: Wakan tanka – the Great Mystery.

In Kabbalah, the name of God that expresses this quality is "Eheieh" – "I am who I am."

IV 20.   The Blessing of the Mandala out of the Center

When you have reached the center, you may want to send out a blessing with the quality of this center into the whole mandala. This may simply be white light, that is radiating outwards from the center, but maybe this blessing may consists also of some words or gestures that seem to be appropriate at that moment.

This is the central act of the whole mandala-ritual and the whole mandala-meditation: To create the mandala anew out of the center – then the quality of the center flows through the mandala out into the world without distortion. The center radiates unhindered outwards as strenght, love, truth and thriving.

IV 21. The Dissolution of the Mandala

When the mandala has been concretely built up on the outside, it may also be dissolved. If the mandala has been made as a stone circle or as an embroidery picture, it will of course remain – but if it has been built up only imaginatively in a ritual or if it has been created out of colored sand on a large table, it will be dissolved again in the end.

The ritual and only imagined mandala is dissolved again by a gesture and possibly some words. The sand of the sand mandala is swept up and possibly scattered into a river.

The inner image of the mandala, however, remains in all cases and is not dissolved – it is put into temporary retirement, so to speak, and then awakened again at the next mandala ceremony.

Sometimes a part of the mandala is also kept and reused in the construction of the next mandala, in order to establish a connection between the two mandala rituals. For example, in the sweat lodge rituals, the small tobacco pouches made for the spirits that hang in the sweat lodge during the ceremony are kept until the next sweat lodge ceremony and then placed in the fire where the stones are heated for the new sweat lodge ceremony.

There are also mandala rituals in which the entire mandala is concretely or imaginatively dissolved toward the end of the ritual. This does not mean the end of the ritual, but an essential part of the ritual itself.

This is a process that is performed at the gate to the innermost ring (area of the deities): In this ring, the continuum is recognized, that is, the lack of delimitation between all things. To reach this realization, sometimes all the complex forms and images of the mandala are dissolved step by step, until in the end only "the one taste in all things" remains.

The purpose of this form of ritual is to enable those who participate in it to experience the continuum. The dissolution of the forms of the mandala is symbolic here of the "leap into the abyss," as which the transition from the ring of the soul to the ring of the deities can be experienced.

IV 22. After the ritual

After the end of the mandala ritual, one is back in everyday life. However, if the mandala ritual has been effective, this everyday life will feel different than before. One will feel the different levels of the world represented by the circle and the four rings in everyday life as well:

- The aliveness of one's own body and one's own presence in the here and now;

- the life force in all things that accompanies one, among other things, as one's own power animal, one's own power plant and one's own power stone and that helps one to heal one's own psyche;

- one's own soul, which gives one support and orientation and which is the source of one's own radiance;

- one's own protective deity, in which one can feel secure at any moment and completely independent of what is happening outside;

- the unity behind all multiplicity, which gives meaning and depth to every single thing and event.

These changes in everyday life and in one's own attitude towards life are the actual goal of every mandala ceremony.

English Books by Harry Eilenstein

- Living Magic (261 p.)	**These books will be puplished soon:**
- The Synthesis of Physics and Magic (192 p.)	- Life Force for Beginners
- Telepathy for Beginners (60 p.)	- Meditation for Beginners
- Telepathy for Advanced Learners (52 p.)	- Kundalini for Beginners
- Telekinesis for Beginners (56 p.)	- Chakra-Magic for Beginners
- Astral Projection for Beginners (60 p.)	- Astrology for Beginners
- Prophecy for Beginners (60 p.)	- Ritual Magic for Beginners
- Invocations for Beginners (52 p.)	- Love Magic for Beginners
- Evocations for Beginners (62 p.)	- Magic Research for Beginners
- Auto-Movement for Beginners (60 p.)	- Symbolism of Numbers for Beginners
- Elves for Beginners (56 p.)	- Language of the Moon – for Beginners
- Hypnosis for Beginners (56 p.)	- Magic Chant for Beginners
- Money Magic for Beginners (60 p.)	- Da'ath-Magic for Beginners
- Magic Objects for Beginners (64 p.)	- Feng Shui for Beginners
- Shamanism for Beginners (52 p.)	- Magic for Beginners – Anthology I
- Self Knowledge for Beginners (60 p.)	- Magic for Beginners – Anthology II
- Number Symbolism for Beginners (64 p.)	- Magic for Beginners – Anthology III
- Mandalas for Beginners (76 p.)	- Magic for Beginners – Anthology IV
- Crop Circles for Beginners (344 p.)	

Bücher von Harry Eilenstein

Religion allgemein	**Germanen**
- Die sieben Schritte des Lebens (428 S.)	- Die Götter der Germanen (87 Bände – siehe nächste Seite)
- Muttergöttin und Schamanen (168 S.)	- Odin (300 S.)
- Göbekli Tepe (472 S.)	**Kelten**
- Die Göttin von Göbekli Tepe (144 S.)	- Cernunnos (690 S.)
- Totempfähle (440 S.)	- Taliesin (228 S.)
- Christus (60 S.)	- Der Kessel von Gundestrup (220 S.)
- Dakini (80 S.)	- Der Chiemsee-Kessel (76)
- Vajra (76 S.)	**Psychologie**
Ägypten	- Über die Freude (100 S.)
- Hathor und Re 1: Götter und Mythen im Alten Ägypten (432 S.)	- Das Geheimnis des inneren Friedens (252 S.)
- Hathor und Re 2: Die altägyptische Religion – Ursprünge, Kult und Magie (396 S.)	- Das Beziehungsmandala (52 S.)
	- Gefühle und ihre Verwandlungen (404 S.)
- Isis (508 S.)	- einsgerichtet (140 S.)
Indogermanen	- Liebe und Eigenständigkeit (216 S.)
- Die Entwicklung der indogermanischen Religionen (700 S.)	- Von innerer Fülle zu äußerem Gedeihen (52 S.)
- Wurzeln und Zweige der indogermanischen Religion (224 S.)	**Heilung**
	- Die Symbolik der Krankheiten (76 S.)
	Kunst
	- Herz des Tanzes – Tanz des Herzens (160 S.)
	Drama
	- König Athelstan (104 S.)

Bücher von Harry Eilenstein

„Magie für Anfänger"

- Telepathie für Anfänger (60 S.)
- Telepathie für Fortgeschrittene (52 S.)
- Telekinese für Anfänger (52 S.)
- Lebenskraft für Anfänger (60 S.)
- Meditation für Anfänger (56 S.)
- Kundalini für Anfänger (100 S.)
- Hypnose für Anfänger (56 S.)
- Auto-Movement für Anfänger (56 S.)
- Chakra-Magie für Anfänger (148 S.)
- Astralreisen für Anfänger (56 S.)
- Astrologie für Anfänger (120 S.)
- Ritual-Magie für Anfänger (56 S.)
- Mandalas für Anfänger (68 S.)
- Geldzauber für Anfänger (56 S.)
- Liebeszauber für Anfänger (52 S.)
- Invokationen für Anfänger (52 S.)
- Evokationen für Anfänger (60 S.)
- Elfen für Anfänger (56 S.)
- Magie-Forschung für Anfänger (140 S.)
- Selbsterkenntnis für Anfänger (52 S.)
- Zahlensymbolik für Anfänger (60 S.)
- Die Sprache des Mondes – für Anfänger (116 S.)
- Zaubergesänge für Anfänger (100 S.)
- Zukunftschau für Anfänger (60 S.)
- Schamanismus für Anfänger (52 S.)
- Magische Gegenstände für Anfänger (68 S.)
- Da'ath-Magie für Anfänger (64 S.)
- Kornkreise für Anfänger (348 S.)
- Feng Shui für Anfänger (96 S.)
- Magie für Anfänger – Sammelband I (696 S.)
- Magie für Anfänger – Sammelband II (664 S.)
- Magie für Anfänger – Sammelband III (580 S.)

„Traumreisen"

- Traumreisen zu Heilpflanzen (700 S.)

Magie

- Handbuch für Zauberlehrlinge (408 S.)
- Tarot (104 S.)
- Physik und Magie (184 S.)
- Die Synthese von Physik und Magie (200S.)
- Die Magie-Formel (156 S.)
- Krafttiere – Tiergöttinnen – Tiertänze (112 S.)
- Schwitzhütten (524 S.)
- Mythen und Magie der Harfe (116 S.)
- Magie heute – Berichte aus der Praxis (288 S.)

Meditation

- Der Lebenskraftkörper (230 S.)
- Die Chakren (100 S.)
- Das Chakren-System mit den Nebenchakren (296 S.)
- Organe und Chakren (64 S.)
- Die platonischen Körper in den Chakren (156 S.)
- Meditation (140 S.)
- Drachenfeuer (124 S.)
- Kundalini I (676 S.)
- Reinkarnation (156 S.)
- eingerichtet (140 S.)

Astrologie

- Astrologie (496 S.)
- Photo-Astrologie (428 S.)
- Die astrologischen Aspekte (88 S.)
- Horoskop und Seele (120 S.)

Kabbala

- Kursus der praktischen Kabbala (150 S.)
- Eltern der Erde (450 S.)
- Blüten des Lebensbaumes:
    - Die Struktur des kabbalistischen Lebensbaumes (370 S.)
    - Der kabbalistische Lebensbaum als Forschungshilfsmittel (580 S.)
    - Der kabbalistische Lebensbaum als spirituelle Landkarte (520 S.)

Die Themen der 87 Bände der Reihe „Die Götter der Germanen"

1. Die Entwicklung der germanischen Religion
2. Lexikon der germanischen Religion
3. Der ursprüngliche Göttervater Tyr
4. Tyr in der Unterwelt: der Schmied Wieland
5. Tyr in der Unterwelt: der Riesenkönig   Teil 1
6. Tyr in der Unterwelt: der Riesenkönig   Teil 2
7. Tyr in der Unterwelt: der Zwergenkönig
8. Der Himmelswächter Heimdall
9. Der Sommergott Baldur
10. Der Meeresgott: Ägir, Hler und Njörd
11. Der Eibengott Ullr
12. Die Zwillingsgötter Alcis
13. Der neue Göttervater Odin   Teil 1
14. Der neue Göttervater Odin   Teil 2
15. Der Fruchtbarkeitsgott Freyr
16. Der Chaos-Gott Loki
17. Der Donnergott Thor
18. Der Priestergott Hönir
19. Die Göttersöhne
20. Die unbekannteren Götter
21. Die Göttermutter Frigg
22. Die Liebesgöttin: Freya und Menglöd
23. Die Erdgöttinnen
24. Die Korngöttin Sif
25. Die Apfel-Göttin Idun
26. Die Hügelgrab-Jenseitsgöttin Hel
27. Die Meeres-Jenseitsgöttin Ran
28. Die unbekannteren Jenseitsgöttinnen
29. Die unbekannteren Göttinnen
30. Die Nornen
31. Die Walküren
32. Die Zwerge
33. Der Urriese Ymir
34. Die Riesen
35. Die Riesinnen
36. Mythologische Wesen
37. Mythologische Priester und Priesterinnen
38. Sigurd/Siegfried
39. Helden und Göttersöhne
40. Die Symbolik der Vögel und Insekten
41. Die Symbolik der Schlangen, Drachen und Ungeheuer
42.a Die Symbolik der Herdentiere I
42.b Die Symbolik der Herdentiere II
43. Die Symbolik der Raubtiere

44. Die Symbolik der Wassertiere und sonstigen Tiere
45. Die Symbolik der Pflanzen
46. Die Symbolik der Farben
47. Die Symbolik der Zahlen
48. Die Symbolik von Sonne, Mond und Sternen
49.a Das Jenseits I – Das Hügelgrab
49.b Das Jenseits II – Der Jenseitsweg
50. Seelenvogel, Utiseta und Einweihung
51. Wiederzeugung und Wiedergeburt
52. Elemente der Kosmologie
53. Der Weltenbaum
54. Die Symbolik der Himmelsrichtungen und der Jahreszeiten
55.a Mythologische Motive I
55.b Mythologische Motive II
56. Der Tempel
57. Die Einrichtung des Tempels
58. Priesterin – Seherin – Zauberin – Hexe
59. Priester – Seher – Zauberer
60. Rituelle Kleidung und Schmuck
61. Skalden und Skaldinnen
62. Kriegerinnen und Ekstase-Krieger
63. Die Symbolik der Körperteile
64.a Magie und Ritual I
64.b Magie und Ritual II
64.c Magie und Ritual III
65. Gestaltwandlungen
66.a Magische Angriffs-Waffen
66.b Magische Verteidigungs-Waffen
67. Magische Werkzeuge und Gegenstände
68. Zaubersprüche
69. Göttermet
70. Zaubertränke
71. Träume, Omen und Orakel
72. Runen
73. Sozial-religiöse Rituale
74. Weisheiten und Sprichworte
75. Kenningar
76. Rätsel
77. Die vollständige Edda des Snorri Sturluson
78. Frühe Skaldenlieder
79.a Mythologische Sagas I
79.b Mythologische Sagas II
80. Hymnen an die germanischen Götter